N. T. WRIGHT
FOR EVERYONE
BIBLE STUDY GUIDES

MATTHEW

25 STUDIES FOR INDIVIDUALS AND GROUPS

N. T. WRIGHT

WITH DALE & SANDY LARSEN

D0047991

IVP Connect

An imprint of InterVarsity Press
Downers Grove, Illinois

InterVarsity Press
P.O. Box 1400, Downers Grove, IL 60515-1426
World Wide Web: www.ivpress.com
E-mail: email@ivpress.com

InterVarsity Press® is the book-publishing division of InterVarsity Christian Fellowship/USA®, a movement of students and faculty active on campus at hundreds of universities, colleges and schools of nursing in the United States of America, and a member movement of the International Fellowship of Evangelical Students. For information about local and regional activities, write Public Relations Dept., InterVarsity Christian Fellowship/USA, 6400 Schroeder Rd., P.O. Box 7895, Madison, WI 53707-7895, or visit the IVCF website at <www.intervarsity.org>.

Cover design: Cindy Kiple
Cover image: xyno/iStockphoto
Interior image: Clipart.com

ISBN 978-0-8308-2181-5

Printed in the United States of America ∞

InterVarsity Press is committed to protecting the environment and to the responsible use of natural resources. As a member of Green Press Initiative we use recycled paper whenever possible. To learn more about the Green Press Initiative, visit <www.greenpressinitiative.org>.

| P | 19 | 18 | 17 | 16 | 15 | 14 |
| Y | 27 | 26 | 25 | 24 | 23 | 22 |

CONTENTS

GETTING THE MOST
OUT OF MATTHEW

Matthew's Gospel presents Jesus in a rich, many-sided way. He appears as the Messiah of Israel, the king who will rule and save the world. He comes before us as the Teacher greater even than Moses. And, of course, he is presented as the Son of Man giving his life for us all. Matthew lays it all out step by step and invites us to learn the wisdom of the gospel message and the new way of life that results from it.

Matthew insists throughout his work that we see in Jesus, even when things are at their darkest, the fulfillment of Scripture. This is how Israel's redeemer was to appear; this is how God would set about liberating his people and bringing justice to the whole world. No point arriving in comfort when the world is in misery; no point having an easy life when the world suffers violence and injustice! If he is to be Emmanuel, God-with-us, he must be with us where the pain is.

God had made promises in the Scriptures of his people, promises of rescue from their many troubles. The Romans had conquered their homeland about sixty years before Jesus was born. They were the most recent of several pagan nations to do so. Israel wanted freedom and looked to God to put everything right. And these promises focused on one thing in particular: God would become king. King not only of Israel but of the whole world. A king who would bring justice and peace at last, who would turn the upside-down world the right way again. There should be no king but God, the revolutionaries believed. God's kingdom, the kingdom of heaven, was what they longed for, prayed for, worked for and were prepared to die for.

But Jesus' contemporaries had many misconceptions to overcome in their view of how Scripture would be fulfilled. God would do all this—and more!—but not in the way they imagined. That is the story Matthew has to tell us. (For more on this fascinating Gospel see my *Matthew for Everyone: Part One* and *Matthew for Everyone: Part Two*, on which this guide is based. Both are published by SPCK and Westminster John Knox.)

As we move through the chapters of Matthew's Gospel in this guide, prepared with the help of Dale and Sandy Larsen, for which I am grateful, we will find a story of danger and hope, of justice and peace. It is a story worth studying.

SUGGESTIONS FOR INDIVIDUAL STUDY

1. As you begin each study, pray that God will speak to you through his Word.

2. Read the introduction to the study and respond to the "Open" question that follows it. This is designed to help you get into the theme of the study.

3. Read and reread the Bible passage to be studied. Each study is designed to help you consider the meaning of the passage in its context. The commentary and questions in this guide are based on my own translation of each passage found in the companion volume to this guide in the For Everyone series on the New Testament (published by SPCK and Westminster John Knox).

4. Write your answers to the questions in the spaces provided or in a personal journal. Each study includes three types of questions: observation questions, which ask about the basic facts in the passage; interpretation questions, which delve into the meaning of the passage; and application questions, which help you discover the implications of the text for growing in Christ. Writing out your responses can bring clarity and deeper understanding of yourself and of God's Word.

5. Each session features selected comments from the For Everyone series. These notes provide further biblical and cultural background and contextual information. They are designed not to answer the questions for you but to help you along as you study the Bible for yourself. For even more reflections on each passage, you may wish to have on hand a copy of the companion volume from the For Everyone series as you work through this study guide.

6. Use the guidelines in the "Pray" section to focus on God, thanking him for what you have learned and praying about the applications that have come to mind.

SUGGESTIONS FOR GROUP MEMBERS

1. Come to the study prepared. Follow the suggestions for individual study mentioned above. You will find that careful preparation will greatly enrich your time spent in group discussion.

2. Be willing to participate in the discussion. The leader of your group will not be lecturing. Instead, she or he will be asking the questions found in this guide and encouraging the members of the group to discuss what they have learned.

3. Stick to the topic being discussed. These studies focus on a particular passage of Scripture. Only rarely should you refer to other portions of the Bible or outside sources. This allows for everyone to participate on equal ground and for in-depth study.

4. Be sensitive to the other members of the group. Listen attentively when they describe what they have learned. You may be surprised by their insights! Each question assumes a variety of answers. Many questions do not have "right" answers, particularly questions that aim at meaning or application. Instead the questions push us to explore the passage more thoroughly.

When possible, link what you say to the comments of others. Also, be affirming whenever you can. This will encourage some of the more hesitant members of the group to participate.

5. Be careful not to dominate the discussion. We are sometimes so eager to express our thoughts that we leave too little opportunity for others to respond. By all means participate! But allow others to also.

6. Expect God to teach you through the passage being discussed and through the other members of the group. Pray that you will have an enjoyable and profitable time together, but also that as a result of the study you will find ways that you can take action individually and/ or as a group.

7. It will be helpful for groups to follow a few basic guidelines. These guidelines, which you may wish to adapt to your situation, should be read at the beginning of the first session.

   • Anything said in the group is considered confidential and will not be discussed outside the group unless specific permission is given to do so.

   • We will provide time for each person present to talk if he or she feels comfortable doing so.

   • We will talk about ourselves and our own situations, avoiding conversation about other people.

   • We will listen attentively to each other.

   • We will be very cautious about giving advice.

Additional suggestions for the group leader can be found at the back of the guide.

THE COMING OF THE KING

Matthew 1:1—2:23

The average modern person who thinks "maybe I'll read the New Testament" is puzzled to find, on the very first page, a long list of names he or she has never heard of. But it is important not to think that this is a waste of time. For many cultures ancient and modern, and certainly in the Jewish world of Matthew's day, this genealogy was the equivalent of a roll of drums, a fanfare of trumpets and a town crier calling for attention. Any first-century Jew would find Jesus' family tree both impressive and compelling. Like a great procession coming down a city street, we watch the figures at the front, and the ones in the middle, but all eyes are waiting for the one who comes in the position of greatest honor, right at the end.

OPEN

When you think of the story of Jesus' birth, what elements immediately come to mind? What mood does it put you in? What questions come to mind?

STUDY

1. *Read Matthew 1:1-17.* In the genealogy of Jesus which names are familiar to you?

2. In the ancient pagan world there were plenty of stories of heroes conceived by the intervention of a god, without a human father. Surely Matthew, with his very Jewish perspective on everything, would hardly invent such a thing, or copy it from someone else unless he really believed it. *Read Matthew 1:18-25.* These extraordinary events bring Joseph face to face with a difficult decision. What personal qualities does he display in the way he handles the situation?

3. When it comes to miracles, are you more skeptical or more ready to believe, and why?

4. Everything depends on whether you believe that the living God could, or would, act in the way Matthew describes. Some say he couldn't ("miracles don't happen"); others that he wouldn't ("if he did that, why doesn't he intervene and stop genocide?"). But Matthew (and Luke) don't ask us to take the story all by itself. They ask us to see it in the light both of the entire history of Israel—in which God was always present and at work, often in very surprising ways—and, more particularly, of the subsequent story of Jesus himself. Does the rest of the story, and the impact of Jesus on the

world and countless individuals within it ever since, make it more or less likely that he was indeed conceived by a special act of the Holy Spirit?

5. What difference do you think it makes, if any, that Jesus was miraculously conceived as the Son of God?

6. *Read Matthew 2:1-12.* Matthew is the only Gospel writer who tells of the visit of the Magi. Think of Christmas pageants, movies and other portrayals you have seen of these events. What familiar elements are—and are not—part of Matthew's account?

7. Herod the Great had no royal blood, and was not even fully Jewish, but was simply an opportunist military commander whom the Romans made into a king to further their own Middle Eastern agendas. Why is Herod so disturbed by what the Magi tell him?

The gifts that the Magi brought were the sort of things that people in the ancient world would think of as appropriate presents to bring to kings, or even gods. What Matthew tells us is political dynamite. Jesus is the true king of the Jews, and old Herod is the false one, a usurper, an imposter.

The arrival of the Magi (who significantly come from a different country) introduces us to something which Matthew wants us to be clear about from the start. If Jesus is in some sense king of the Jews, that doesn't mean that his rule is limited to the Jewish people. At the heart of many prophecies about the coming king, the Messiah, there were predictions that his rule would bring God's justice and peace to the whole world (Psalm 72; Isaiah 11:1-10). Matthew will end his Gospel with Jesus commissioning his followers to go out and make disciples from every nation; this, it seems, is the way that the prophecies of the Messiah's worldwide rule are going to come true.

8. *Read Matthew 2:13-23.* What were results of political power and ambition being threatened?

9. At the heart of the Christmas story in Matthew's Gospel is a baby who poses such a threat to the most powerful man around that he kills a whole village full of other babies in order to try to get rid of him. In fact the shadow of the cross falls over the story from this moment on. Jesus is born with a price on his head.

   In what ways do you see God at work throughout Matthew 1—2?

10. The gospel of Jesus the Messiah was born in a land and at a time of trouble, tension, violence and fear. Banish all thoughts of peaceful Christmas scenes. Before the Prince of Peace had learned to walk and talk, he was a homeless refugee with a price on his head. At the same time, Matthew insists that we see in Jesus, even when things are at their darkest, the fulfillment of Scripture. This is how Israel's

redeemer was to appear; this is how God would set about liberating his people and bringing justice to the whole world. If he is to be Emmanuel, God-with-us, he must be with us where the pain is.

What comes to your mind when you think of "where the pain is" in your community, in your family, in your church, in the world?

11. How do the first two chapters of Matthew speak to this pain?

12. Matthew's Gospel has stood at the front of the New Testament since very early times. Millions of Christians have read the genealogy as the beginning of their own exploration of who Jesus was and is. Once we understand what it all means, we are ready to proceed with the story. This, Matthew is saying, is *both* the fulfillment of two millennia of God's promises and purposes *and* something quite new and different. God still works like that today: keeping his promises, acting in character, and yet always ready with surprises for those who learn to trust him.

What surprises have you found in the beginning of this study of Matthew?

PRAY

Offer prayers of thanks to Jesus because he did not stand aloof from our world. Pray about those areas you identified where Jesus can once again enter into times and places of pain, conflict and danger.

NOTE ON MATTHEW 1:1-17

Matthew has arranged the names so as to make a clear point. Most Jews, telling the story of Israel's ancestry, would begin with Abraham; but only a select few, by the first century A.D., would trace their own line through King David. Even fewer would be able to continue by going on through Solomon and the other kings of Judah all the way to the exile. Israel had no functioning monarchy for most of the several hundred years after that. Some Israelites at this time knew, however, that they were descended from the line of true and ancient kings. Even to tell that story, to list those names, was therefore making a political statement. You wouldn't want Herod's spies to overhear you boasting that you were part of the true royal family.

Matthew arranges the genealogy into three groups of fourteen names—or, perhaps we should say, into six groups of seven names. The number seven was and is one of the most powerful symbolic numbers, and to be born at the beginning of the seventh seven, as Jesus was, is clearly to be the climax of the whole list.

The markers along the way tell their own story of promises made (to Abraham), of many promises fulfilled (in David) and of further promises seemingly lost (in Babylon). Now all the promises would be complete in this child.

JOHN AND JESUS

Matthew 3:1-17

About sixty years before Jesus was born, the Romans conquered his homeland. They were the last in a long line of pagan nations to do so. They had installed Herod the Great and then his sons after him as puppet monarchs to do their dirty work for them. Most Jews resented both parts of this arrangement and longed for a chance to revolt.

But the Jews weren't just eager for freedom in the way that most subject peoples are. They wanted it because of what they believed about God, themselves and the world. If there was one God who had made the whole world, and if they were his special people, then it couldn't be God's will to have pagan foreigners ruling them. What's more, God had made promises in their scriptures that one day he would rescue them and put everything right. These promises focused on one thing in particular: God would become king, not only of Israel but of the whole world. But that hadn't happened yet. No political or military leader had rid the land of the hated conquerors as they expected and hoped for. Obviously something was still wrong.

OPEN

If the president or prime minister were scheduled to visit your house, how would you prepare for the visit?

STUDY

1. *Read Matthew 3:1-17.* What is the heart of John's message?

2. What role had the Jordan played in Israel's history many hundreds of years earlier? (See, for example, Numbers 33:48-56 and Deuteronomy 11:8-15.)

3. What is similar and different this time as John has people passing through the Jordan?

4. John was plunging the people who came to him in the wilderness in the water of the river Jordan as they confessed their sins. This wasn't just a symbolic cleansing for individuals; it was a sign of the new thing that God was doing in history, for Israel and for the world. Over a thousand years before, the children of Israel had crossed the Jordan when they first entered and conquered the Promised Land. Now they had to go through the river again, as a sign that they were getting ready for a greater conquest, God's defeat of all evil and the establishment of his kingdom on earth as in heaven.

   Not only did ordinary people come to hear John, so did some Jewish religious leaders, the Pharisees and Sadducees. Why does John speak to them so harshly?

5. What particular dangers are there for those who have leadership responsibilities in the church?

6. In particular, John attacks the confidence the Jewish leaders had in their ancestry. "We have Abraham as our father," they would say to themselves. In other words, "God made promises to Abraham; we are his children; therefore God is committed to us, and we are bound to be all right in the end."

Most of us aren't ethnically Jewish. But what sorts of equivalent confidence might we in the church claim to have today that might be equally fruitless?

7. You may think that your house is reasonably tidy and well kept, but if you suddenly get word that the king is coming to visit, you may suddenly want to give it another cleaning. The Jewish people, even the devout ones who worshiped regularly in the temple, knew in their bones that they weren't ready for God to come back. The prophets had said that God would come back when the people repented, turning to him with all their hearts. That was what John summoned them to do; and they came in droves. John's stark warnings set the tone for much of the story of Jesus.

The God who came to his people in Jesus will one day unveil his kingdom in all its glory, bringing justice and joy to the whole world. If you knew this was to happen next year, what changes would you want to make in the world before he came? Figuratively, where do the roads need straightening out? What fires need to be lit to burn away the rubbish in his path? Which dead trees need to be cut down?

8. In the next year, what steps could you and your Christian community make toward those desires?

9. Why would Jesus come to be baptized? What good will this do and how will it bring about the result that John and his hearers are longing for?

10. Jesus' baptism surprises us, even today. He will fulfill God's righteous plan to rescue God's people from every kind of exile, but not in the way we expect. He will humbly identify himself with God's people, take their place, share their repentance, live their life and ultimately die their death.

How is the fulfillment of all this hinted at in what happens when Jesus comes up out of the water?

11. Part of the challenge of this passage is to learn afresh to be surprised by Jesus. He comes to fulfill God's plans, not ours. How does Jesus surprise then and now?

How do our sometimes minor concerns compare with God's plans?

PRAY

Ask God what you and your community need to repent of. Pray that you will be able to follow through on steps to prepare your world now for the justice God will be bringing.

3

Announcing the Kingdom

Matthew 4:1-25

After winning the election to the legislature, Jennifer was elated but exhausted and needed time to think. Her dreams of service, of changing the world, were still there but she was surprised by other voices. "Now at last," they whispered, "you've got a chance to make some real money. And if you play your cards well, don't make a fuss and get to know the right people, you could be on the road to higher office and fame. And you know that party activist you've never liked. You've got power. Now's the time to get rid of him."

OPEN

How and why are the ideals people have often compromised over time?

STUDY

1. One early Christian writer tells us that Jesus was tempted like other humans in every possible way (Hebrews 4:15). We should not be surprised that after his great moment of vision, when his sense of

God's calling and love was so dramatically confirmed at his baptism, Jesus had to face the whispering voices of temptation and recognize them for what they are. *Read Matthew 4:1-11.*

How do the temptations play on Jesus' being the Son of God (see 3:17)?

2. The devil offers several means for Jesus to achieve his goals. What are these means that Jesus rejects?

3. The temptations we all face, day by day and at critical moments of decision and vocation in our lives, may be very different from those of Jesus, but they have exactly the same point. They are not simply trying to entice us into committing this or that sin. They are trying to distract us, to turn us aside, from the path of servanthood to which our baptism has commissioned us.

What calling or purpose has he given his followers, and how are we distracted from that so often?

4. We are entitled to use the same defense as God's Son himself. We can store Scripture in our hearts and know how to use it.

How has Scripture helped you meet temptation or kept you from being distracted from God's purposes?

The biblical texts Jesus used as his key weapons are all taken from the story of Israel in the wilderness. Jesus had come through the waters of baptism, like Israel crossing the Red Sea. He now had to face, in forty days and nights in the wilderness, the equivalent of Israel's forty years in the desert. But where Israel failed its tests again and again, Jesus succeeded. Here at last is a true Israelite, Matthew is saying. He has come to do what God always wanted Israel to do—to bring light to the world (see v. 16).

5. *Read Matthew 4:12-17.* Matthew's Gospel usually speaks of the "kingdom of heaven"; the other Gospels normally use the phrase "kingdom of God." Saying *heaven* instead of *God* was a regular Jewish way of avoiding the word *God* out of reverence and respect. Matthew was therefore not talking about the place where God's people go after their death. It meant, as Jesus' listeners at the time understood, God's rule here on earth.

In what sense could this kingdom be said to be "approaching" or "arriving"?

6. The word *repent* is also open to misunderstanding. Many think it means "feeling bad about yourself." It means instead "change direction" or "turn around and go the other way." How you *feel* about it isn't really the important thing. It's what you *do* that matters.

The main problem for Israel at the time was that God's kingdom was not in place. Rome's was. Israel wanted to get rid of it, and had fought and killed to do so for almost two centuries. Yet as we saw in Jesus' responses to the temptations in 4:1-11, he rejected power, privilege and glory as a way to advance his agenda.

In verses 15-16, Matthew now quotes from Isaiah 9:1-7. How is he saying that Israel needs to repent and change direction?

7. How might changing direction and receiving God's kingdom go hand in hand for us?

8. *Read Matthew 4:18-25.* What strikes you about how Simon, Andrew, James and John respond to Jesus?

9. Do you know of someone who set aside a promising or lucrative opportunity to take a job or follow a career because of Christian values or convictions? If so, describe the situation.

10. Sometimes Jesus' call comes slowly, starting like a faint murmur. Sometimes he calls people as suddenly and dramatically as he called Peter and Andrew, James and John. How and what first drew you to Jesus?

11. Why did people back then give up everything to follow a wandering preacher? Why do people today give up lifestyles and practices that look attractive and lucrative in order to maintain honesty, integrity, faith, hope and love? The answer can only be in Jesus himself and in the astonishing magnetism of his presence and personality. We can feel it today as we meditate on the stories about him and pray to know him better, just as the first disciples knew and felt his presence 2,000 years ago.

The fishermen by the Sea of Galilee had no idea where following Jesus would lead them. How has being a disciple taken you in unexpected directions or turned out differently from the way you expected?

12. In times of difficulty, what has kept you following Jesus?

PRAY

Pray that you will keep or regain your first sense of what drew you to Jesus. Pray about particular temptations you face, and ask God to reveal strategies to combat them.

4

WORDS FROM
A MOUNTAINSIDE

Matthew 5:1-48

This passage is the beginning of the Sermon on the Mount (Matthew 5—7), which sets out the main themes of Jesus' proclamation. People often say what a wonderful teaching the Sermon on the Mount is, and that if only people would obey it the world would be a better place. But if we think of Jesus simply sitting there telling people how to behave properly, we will miss what was really going on. These *blessings,* the *wonderful news* that he's announcing, are not saying "Try hard to live like this." They are saying that people who already *are* like this are in good shape. They should be happy and celebrate.

OPEN

What enemies do you know of, whether individuals or groups, who have reconciled? If you can't think of any instances, why do you think reconciliation is rare?

STUDY

1. *Read Matthew 5:1-12.* The first word of each verse in 5:3-11 is tra-

ditionally translated "Blessed" or "Happy." This list is sometimes called *the Beatitudes* because the Latin word *beatus* means "blessed." Jesus is not suggesting that these are simply timeless truths about the way the world is. If he was saying that, he was wrong. Mourners often go uncomforted, and those who long for justice frequently take that longing to the grave. Jesus is saying that with his work these things start to come true. This is an announcement, not a philosophical analysis of the world. It is gospel—an announcement of wonderful news, of good news, not good advice.

What would be "wonderful news" for most people in your society?

love, support, honesty, kindness

2. What would be "wonderful news" for you?

that the Lord will receive me and forgive my sins.

"Follow me," Jesus said to the first disciples, because in him the living God was doing a new thing. This list of *wonderful news* is part of his invitation, part of his summons, part of his way of saying that God is at work in a fresh way and this is what it looks like.

3. *Read Matthew 5:13-20.* How does Isaiah 42:6-7 help us understand what Jesus is getting at in 5:14-15?

To be the light on the mountain to shine before man and to be the light that guides us.

4. In what practical ways do Christians serve as "salt" and "light" in the world?

to let the light shine before men that they may see the good deeds and praise our Father in Heaven.

5. How is Jesus himself a fulfillment of 5:13-20?

*He has shone us the
right that it may shine
to everybody*

Israel was not chosen in order to be God's special people while the rest
of the world remained in outer darkness. Jerusalem, a city set on a hill,
was to be a beacon of hope for the world. Israel was chosen to be the
salt of the earth, so that, through Israel, God could bless all people.
Now Jesus was calling Israel to *be* the light of the world at last.
Jesus wasn't intending to abandon the law and the prophets. Israel's whole story—commands, promises and all—was to come true
in him. Now that he was here, a way was opening up for Israel and
all the world to make God's covenant a reality in their own selves,
changing behavior not just by teaching but by a change of heart and
mind itself.

6. In the next section of the Sermon on the Mount, Jesus takes the commands of the law and shows how they provide a blueprint for a way
of being fully, genuinely, gloriously human. This new way, which
Jesus had come to pioneer and make possible, goes deep down into
the roots of personality and produces a different pattern of behavior
altogether. *Read Matthew 5:21-26.*

According to Jesus' words here, reconciliation comes prior even to
worship. As his alternative to anger and violence, Jesus offers two
remarkably specific and practical commands. Be reconciled; make
friends. How simple that is, and yet how hugely difficult and costly!
What are some possible costs of being reconciled and making friends
with an enemy?

*be influenced to 'give in'
rather than truly reconcile
and forgive.*

7. What has helped you to reconcile with others and make friends?

*It is a different process / task
to forgive and to show an open
hand when your adversary will not*

8. *Read Matthew 5:27-37.* This passage mentions divorce between two other issues. How do they relate to the issue of divorce?

Jesus says clearly, deal ruthlessly with the first signs of lust. Plucking out eyes and cutting off hands are deliberate exaggerations, but they make the point very forcibly. Don't suppose Jesus means you must never feel the impulse of lust, which is impossible; that's not what the words mean. He commands us to avoid the extended gaze and the lustful imagination that follow the initial impulse. Choosing not to be swept along by inappropriate sexual passion may well feel on occasion like cutting off a hand—and our world has frequently tried to tell us that doing this is very bad for us. But, for neither the first nor the last time, we must choose to obey our Lord rather than the world.

9. Jesus' comments about speech and swearing appear to be a deepening of the second commandment, not to take the Lord's name in vain. Most things people regularly swore by in the casual speech of the day could be traced back to God. What sort of damage is done when people don't tell the truth or when they make inflated promises?

10. *Read Matthew 5:38-48.* If we follow Jesus' commands, how will we surprise our enemies?

11. Jesus called Israel to fulfill these verses in their own context. How does Jesus fulfill them himself?

12. The examples Jesus gives are only little sketches to give you the idea. Whatever situation you are in, you need to think it through for yourself. Despite pressure and provocation, despite your own anger and frustration, what would it mean for you to reflect God's generous love? Consider specific people and situations.

PRAY

Matthew 5, the first part of the Sermon on the Mount, covers many intense issues. Which of Jesus' statements makes you most uncomfortable? Thank God for speaking to your conscience. Pray that you will know the transformation of Christ in that area of your life.

NOTE ON MATTHEW 5:31-32

This passage is not, of course, the only place in the New Testament where the matter of divorce comes up. It is important to study Mark 10:2-12, Luke 16:18 and 1 Corinthians 7:10-16, as well as this passage and Matthew 19:3-9. Together they show both that Jesus set his face firmly against divorce (in line with Old Testament teaching; e.g., Malachi 2:14-15) and that the first-century church wrestled with how to apply this in practice.

For Matthew, here and in chapter 19, sexual immorality by one partner—presumably an adulterous relationship of some kind—is sufficient grounds for divorce. For Paul, if a Christian is married to a non-Christian, and the non-Christian wants to separate, that too is sufficient; though he insists, despite what some in his churches may well have felt and wanted, that the Christian should not initiate the split. And it seems clear to me (though not to all writers on this subject) that in both these cases divorce is only divorce if it allows for remarriage. To put that the other way round: if one is not allowed to remarry, then divorce has not really taken place. So if in these two cases divorce is clearly allowed, we must assume that remarriage is at least potentially envisaged.

PIETY AND PRAYER

Matthew 6:1-34

Facing his professor, the student looked crestfallen, as well he might. For weeks he had thought he was doing all right. Yes, he hadn't been working as hard as he could have; but he was part of the college football team, and he was playing in a rock group, and he was reading some very exciting novels . . . and somehow he hadn't been spending quite as much time in the library as most of the others. Now his professor was asking him, What were his priorities? Did he want an education, a job or just a good time?

OPEN

What motivates you or gives you energy for some activity or goal?

STUDY

1. *Read Matthew 6:1-18.* Jesus doesn't say we should refrain from giving money, praying or fasting. He assumes that people will continue to

do all of these. He's concerned about how we do them. What does he say about all three regarding motive?

2. Jesus doesn't say we shouldn't be interested in rewards. In fact, three times (vv. 4, 6 and 18) he says that God will repay. What do you think he has in mind?

3. Jesus says that when you give money away, it is best simply to try to forget about it. Sometimes donated money is used as a way for people to get what they want or accomplish what they think is best in a church or charitable organization. How does 6:1-4 apply to this sort of situation?

4. In 6:5-8 Jesus describes how people make a show of prayer. How might people do the same today?

5. Jesus contrasts the sort of praying he has in mind with the sort that went on in much of the non-Jewish world at that time. We know from many writings and inscriptions that they used many formulas with long, complicated magic words they would repeat over and over in their anxiety to persuade some god or goddess to be favorable to them. Jesus instead provides a framework for prayer.

What are the key elements in the structure he provides?

6. What do the first half (vv. 9-10) and the second half (vv. 11-13) of the prayer focus on?

7. What does this tell us about how we should pray?

8. After the prayer, Jesus comments that the heart that will not open to forgive others will remain closed when God's own forgiveness is offered. (He'll say more about this in chapter 18.) How does this strike you?

9. *Read Matthew 6:19-34.* How does this passage emphasize priorities in different ways?

10. How are the discussions of money and worry related?

11. When Jesus tells us not to worry about what to eat or drink or wear, he doesn't mean that these things don't matter. He doesn't mean that we should prefer to eat and drink as little as possible. The point was priorities. Nor does Jesus mean, of course, that we should not plant seeds and reap harvests or work to make clothes. Rather if we set aside worry and aim at God's priorities, food, drink and clothing look after themselves.

Why is worry so difficult to set aside in favor of God's priorities?

12. When Jesus told his followers not to worry about tomorrow, we must assume he led them by example. He seems to have had the skill of living totally in the present, giving attention totally to the present task, celebrating the goodness of God here and now. If that's not a recipe for happiness, I don't know what is.

How do you respond to the idea that Jesus was basically a happy person?

13. What is one thing you can do this week to start learning his skill of living in the present?

PRAY

Pray the prayer found in 6:9-13, elaborating on and filling in each element found there.

6

WARNING SIGNS

Matthew 7:1-29

Driving the car these days near where I live becomes more and more complicated each day. On any given stretch of road there are more and more warning signs. "Lane closed." "Mud on Road." "Slow Farm Vehicles." Not to mention signs telling you how fast you're allowed to drive, warning you there are police cameras waiting to catch you if you speed, suggesting you stop for a cup of coffee before you get too tired and telling you how far it is to your destination. Jesus ends the great Sermon on the Mount with a set of warning signs.

OPEN

What warnings or warning signs that you received do you wish you had taken heed of?

STUDY

1. *Read Matthew 7:1-6.* Jesus isn't saying that there is no such thing as public morality. He is not referring to official law courts. God

intends that his world should be ordered, and that injustice should be held in check. Rather, Jesus is referring to the judgments and condemnations that occur within ordinary lives. He is warning that the very people who seem most eager to tell others what to do (or not to do) are the people who should take a long look in the mirror before they begin.

How would you and your Christian community look if people were less eager to point out "specks" in the eyes of other people and were more aware of the "planks" in their own?

2. God is like an artist working with difficult material. Prayer is the way some of that material cooperates with the artist instead of resisting him. *Read Matthew 7:7-12.* What do we learn about God's character here?

3. How does this affect your attitude toward 7:7-8?

4. Jesus isn't suggesting that we ask God for the wrong sorts of things. The problem is perhaps that we are not nearly eager enough to ask for the right things.

   Consider whether you find it easy or difficult to bring your requests to God about anything and everything. What experiences have shaped your attitude toward praying?

5. Archbishop William Temple famously said, "When I pray, coincidences happen; when I stop praying, the coincidences stop happening." Does that match your experience or not? Explain.

6. Jesus is neither the first nor the last great moral teacher to offer this so-called golden rule found in verse 12. How does the content of verse 12 connect the thoughts preceding it in 7:9-11?

7. *Read Matthew 7:13-23.* This passage has three warnings—about narrow gates, false prophets and a day of judgment—that each describe two different ways one could follow. What help do each of these three have to offer us to make sure we are following the right way?

8. How in our community can we recognize good fruit and good trees on the one hand and bad fruit and bad trees on the other without being guilty of the judgment Jesus warns about in verses 1-6?

9. *Read Matthew 7:24-29.* At the end of this passage, in 7:28, Matthew rounds off the long Sermon on the Mount by commenting, "So, when Jesus had finished these words . . ." If we are observant in the chapters to come, we will find similar statements about Jesus finishing some teaching in Matthew 11:1, 13:53, 19:1 and 26:1. This is how Matthew has marked off the five great blocks of teaching in his Gospel. In this way Matthew echoes the Old Testament. And as every Jew knew, the first five books of the Bible were known as "the five books of Moses." One of the main things Matthew wants to tell us is that Jesus is like Moses—only more so.

As you consider Matthew 5—7, how would Matthew want his readers to understand that Jesus is similar to but greater than Moses?

10. When Jesus therefore insists in 7:24-27 that his listeners will be judged on whether they hear his words and do them, it is, he says, the difference between a house that stays standing in a storm and a house that falls with a great crash.

How can our church or Christian community build a "house" that will stand?

11. Not far away in Jerusalem, Herod's men were continuing to rebuild the temple. They spoke of it as God's House and declared that it was built upon the rock. In the last of Jesus' five sermons in Matthew (23—25), Jesus warns that the temple itself will come crashing down because Israel as a whole had failed to respond to Jesus' message. Because they have failed to be the light on the hill, to reject

open violence and rebellion, and to make friends with their enemies, a national catastrophe would befall them, which in fact it did in A.D. 70 when the temple was destroyed by the Romans.

Jesus had a very specific promise and warning for his own people in his own day. But this message is also for us, encouraging us to build our lives on Jesus' words and to be part of a house that lasts forever.

What teaching has stuck with you most from Matthew 5—7?

12. We could suggest that a title for the whole Sermon on the Mount might be "What it means to call God 'Father.'" What new insights about your relationship with the Father have you gained from studying the Sermon on the Mount?

PRAY

Thank God that he is the loving father described in 7:9-10. Ask God for the things you think a loving father would delight to give his children.

Spoken with Authority

Matthew 8:1—9:8

There is nothing in the New Testament to suggest that *faith* is a general awareness of a supernatural dimension or a general trust in the goodness of some distant divinity. Nor does it suggest that some might arrive at faith through Jesus or equally through others by some quite different route. *Faith*, in Christian terms, means believing precisely that the living God has entrusted his authority to Jesus himself, who is now exercising it for the salvation of the world.

OPEN

What do people you know—friends, neighbors, family, coworkers—say about authority? How do they (and you) respond to it?

STUDY

1. *Read Matthew 8:1-13. Leprosy* (the word covered several types of vir-

ulent skin diseases) meant not only sickness and disfigurement, but also social banishment.

How does Jesus restore the leper as a full member of God's people?

2. The centurion's faith amazes Jesus. How is the faith of the centurion different from what Jesus has seen so far in others?

3. What does it mean to recognize and submit to the authority of Jesus today, to call him *Lord* and live by that?

4. *Read Matthew 8:14-22*. How does Matthew connect the healing Jesus offered during his life and the healing he offered through his own suffering and death?

5. Jesus seems to discourage one would-be follower and then prod another into following. What do these two have in common?

"The son of man" (8:20) is a very cryptic phrase also found in Daniel 7:13-14; it could simply mean "I" or "someone like me." But for Matthew, who knows several other sayings in which this strange phrase occurs, there is no question: it carries the note of authority (see for example Matthew 9:6 and 26:64). But it also speaks of suffering (Matthew 20:28).

According to the rabbis, when a man's father dies he has a strong obligation to give him a proper burial. Of course, we don't know if the man's father here had actually died yet. The man may have been using his future obligation as a way of postponing following Jesus. The response Jesus offers means that what he, Jesus, was doing was so important, so urgent, so immediate that whatever else you were thinking of doing, this comes first.

6. *Read Matthew 8:23-27.* Unlike their neighbors to the north and south (Phoenicia and Egypt), the Jews (except for fishermen) were not as a whole a seafaring people. They concentrated on the land, which was after all their promised inheritance. In Jewish writing the sea remained a place and a power of darkness and evil, threatening and wild.

How does this background help explain the disciples' terror and their awe of Jesus?

7. It's all very well to say in church or in private devotion that Jesus is the Son of God, the Lord, the Messiah or whatever. Matthew wants us to ask ourselves, Do we actually treat him as if he has authority over every aspect of our lives and our world?

In what ways does he make a difference in our day-to-day lives?

8. *Read Matthew 8:28-34.* What strikes you most about what the demons cry out, and why?

9. After Jesus has quieted the storm, the disciples ask one another what sort of man he can be. Now we get an answer. The phrase "son of God" is also used later in Matthew and most likely refers to Jesus as Messiah, the one who would judge the world and set all things right.

   Why do you think the local people beg Jesus to leave?

10. *Read Matthew 9:1-8.* How does the authority which Jesus claims in this passage go beyond any that he has demonstrated so far?

11. What do the different episodes in Matthew 8:1—9:8 have in common? How do they contrast with one another?

12. How does Jesus' authority throughout Matthew 8:1—9:8 contrast with how we typically see authority exercised?

13. As Matthew asks his readers (including us) to follow Jesus, we need to know that Jesus isn't just somebody with good ideas. He isn't just somebody who will tell us how to establish a better relationship with God. He is somebody with authority over everything that the physical world on the one hand, and the nonphysical world on the other, can throw at us. This is a Jesus we can trust with every aspect of our lives.

In what areas of your life do you need to put trust in the authority of Christ?

PRAY

Thank the Lord for the ways he has proved he is trustworthy. Pray for the courage to yield all areas of your life to his authority.

NOTE ON MATTHEW 8:28-34

Today we struggle, in the modern Western world, to explain what's going on inside people like the men described here. In Jesus' world, and in many parts of our world today, the most natural explanation is that some evil force or forces has taken them over. "Demons," and possession by such creatures, was the regular way of describing that condition. Modern Western medicine has found alternative diagnoses for many people in this turbulent state; but there remain some for whom the ancient explanation still seems to be the best.

Everywhere else Jesus went, people asked him to stay with them, and brought him more sick people to cure. Curiously, the people of Gadara regarded him with fear, and begged him to leave their district. Was it because they were Gentiles, and were anxious about the Jewish Messiah coming to them? Was it because they were frightened that if he started sending pigs into the lake he might cause other destruction of property and livestock? We don't know. What we do know is that he was a force to be reckoned with.

8

A New World Coming

Matthew 9:9—10:42

Those of us who live in the Western world take it for granted that we live in a tolerant society. We don't expect people to haul us off into court for what we believe. We don't expect to be beaten up because we speak about Jesus. We certainly don't expect to find ourselves coming before governors and monarchs on a charge of treason. But Jesus' message was truly revolutionary, and like all true revolutionaries he and his followers were regarded as very dangerous. Jesus knew that his message was opposed to the agendas his contemporaries were following, particularly those who were eager for violent revolution against Rome.

OPEN

What have you learned about good and bad ways of dealing with opposition?

STUDY

1. Jesus came not to destroy but to fulfill. God's new world was being born, and from now on everything would be different. In the middle of all this newness sits a surprised and grateful man, Matthew, tell-

ing the story of his own calling as the tax collector, who had been lumped together with sinners for being a collaborator with the occupying Roman force. *Read Matthew 9:9-31.*

Jesus uses three word pictures in 9:14-17 to tell John's disciples what is going on. What do the images have in common?

2. In societies before modern medicine, it was vital to have strict codes about what you could and couldn't touch, and what to do if you did contract impurity. The regulations were and are practical wisdom to keep society in good shape. For the Jewish people two of the things that were near the top of the list were dead bodies and women with internal bleeding, including menstrual periods.

    How does Jesus deal with the two people who would have made him "unclean"?

3. What sorts of "uncleanness" do you see in your own culture, and how can you approach it in the spirit of Christ?

4. In 9:27-37, what do you think is behind the Pharisees' accusation that Jesus is in league with "the prince of demons," that is, Satan?

5. Outside the Lord's Prayer itself, Jesus doesn't often tell his followers what to pray for, but in 9:35-38 he does. Jesus expected his disciples to be the answer to their own prayer, as he might expect of us. What

do you find yourself praying about often or intensely, and how might God use you as part of the answer to those prayers?

6. Up until this time, the disciples have been like passengers in a car while Jesus has been doing all the driving. Now he is about to tell them to go off and do it themselves. Here for the first time Matthew calls them *apostles* or people who are "sent out." *Read Matthew 10:1-31.*

Imagine that you are one of the apostles, about to set out on the mission Jesus has given you. What is the most urgent question you want to ask him before you leave?

7. The instructions Jesus gives in 10:1-15 are very specific, for a particular situation. But Matthew has recorded them in detail, presumably because he thinks they remain relevant to the church even after Jesus' death and resurrection. How might they apply to the mission of your church?

8. Matthew has already noted how foreign dignitaries honored Jesus at his birth (2:1-2) and that Gentiles would come flooding into the kingdom (8:11). Soon he will send the disciples out to all the nations (28:19). For now, however, there is an urgent and immediate task. Israel itself must hear the message and must be given a chance to repent before it's too late. For the moment, every effort must be made to tell the chosen people that their great moment, the fulfillment of their dreams, has arrived. The apostles were to be healers, restorers, people who will bring life and hope to others, showing what kind of kingdom was coming, rushing upon Israel like an express train, and they had to get ready for it.

In 10:16-23 there is a dramatic shift from the excitement of sharing some of Jesus' own extraordinary power to dire warnings of trouble and persecution. In such a context, what do you think it means to be "as shrewd as snakes, and as innocent as doves"?

9. What happens when Christians lean too much one way or the other, toward innocence or toward shrewdness?

10. On what basis does Jesus tell his followers not to be afraid in 10:24-31?

If God really takes note of every single sparrow in the sky and every single hair of our heads, then just as nothing is too great for him to do, nothing is too small for him to care about. Followers of Jesus are bound to expect attacks at all levels. But they should also learn that the one they are serving is stronger than the strongest opponent they will ever meet.

11. *Read Matthew 10:32-42.* Some have misguidedly taken passages like Matthew 10:32-42 as a license to neglect their own dependents and spend all their time on "the Lord's work." Jesus did not want to bring division within households for the sake of it; but he knew that if people followed his way, division was bound to follow. He is to have priority over all other relationships.

What does this passage say about allegiances and priorities?

12. What does Jesus say about rewards?

13. Jesus calls on his followers to care for each other at many levels. How can we do this?

PRAY

Where are the fields today that look like they're ready for harvest? Pray that the Lord will send more workers to harvest those fields. Pray about how you might be part of the answer to your own prayer.

NOTE ON MATTHEW 10:28-31

Why would Jesus tell his followers not to be afraid, then to *be* afraid, then *not* to be afraid again, all in the space of a few sentences? Jesus believed that Israel was faced in his day by enemies at two quite different levels. There were the obvious ones: Rome, Herod and their underlings. They were the ones who had the power to kill the body. But there were other, darker enemies, who had the power to kill the soul as well. The demonic powers might use the desire of God's people for justice and vengeance as the bait on a hook. The people of light are never more at risk than when they are lured into fighting the darkness with more darkness. So their concern should not be with losing a political or military fight. Rather they should fear losing the spiritual battle by using the ways of darkness.

Some people think that when Jesus urges us to fear the one who can destroy body and soul in hell, he is referring to God himself. But the point here is the opposite. God is the one we do *not* have to fear. Indeed, he is the one we can trust with our lives, our souls, our bodies, everything.

9

NOT AS EXPECTED

Matthew 11:1-30

Throughout the eleventh chapter of Matthew, Jesus is dealing with the fact that what he is doing is not what people expect him to do. He knows it, is facing it and believes that this is the way to go, the way to bring in God's kingdom even though it isn't what others had imagined. John the Baptist even sent messengers to ask him "Are you the one who is coming?" The answer is, yes and no. Jesus believed that he really was the Messiah. But he had rewritten a key bit of the play, to the surprise and consternation of the other actors and the audience. He was going back to a different script and a different kind of story.

OPEN

When has God not done things the way you expected? How has your understanding of God grown and changed through these surprise experiences?

STUDY

1. Jesus' cousin John the Baptist seems to have expected Jesus to be a man of fire who would sweep through Israel as Elijah had dealt with

the prophets of Baal. Now, in prison, John was disappointed and having doubts. *Read Matthew 11:1-30.*

What evidence does Jesus present for who he is in verses 1-6?

2. People would recognize that Jesus comes in the tradition of Old Testament prophets. Yet he says he is bringing mercy to sinners. Why would anyone be upset by what Jesus was doing (v. 6)? What might they think he should be bringing instead?

3. As Jesus speaks to the crowds in verses 7-15, what does he tell them about John and therefore indirectly about himself?

4. How is it possible that the "least significant person in heaven's kingdom" (v. 11) is greater than John the Baptist?

5. Jesus paid John the Baptist a very great compliment but also said that the time for that sort of work had come to an end. The kingdom of heaven was now breaking in. The whole sweep and swathe of history that led up to John and his work was now being wound up, not because it was a failure but because it was a success.

Look at Matthew 11:16-24. How are John and Jesus the targets of different kinds of accusations?

6. Jesus had lived in Capernaum. He knew Chorazin and Bethsaida, nearby towns just a short walk along the lakeside. Why does Jesus pronounce such judgment against these towns?

7. Jesus offered a last chance to embrace a kingdom vision different from violent revolution, a revolution against Rome that they were destined to lose. He had outlined it in his great sermon and the teaching he was giving in towns and villages all over Galilee. He was living it out on the street and in houses filled with laughter and friendship. With his healings he was showing how powerful it was. And people didn't want it—and they were ready to use any excuse to avoid the issue.

What excuses do people use today to avoid the issue of the kingdom of God?

8. For the average Jew of Jesus' day, *wisdom* was about as far out of reach as being a brain surgeon or a test pilot is for most people today. You needed to be a scholar, trained in languages and literature, with leisure to ponder and discuss weighty and complicated matters.

In Matthew 11:25-30, how does Jesus slice through all the barriers to acquiring wisdom?

9. Jesus suggests that the true God can be known only through him. How does Jesus put a warm and welcoming face on this prospect?

10. What have you learned about Jesus so far in Matthew that sheds light on who God is?

11. How have you found verses 28-30 to be true in your own experience?

12. Mercy was at the heart of Jesus' messianic mission, just as it remains at the heart of the church's work today. Whether or not it's the script people want us to follow, it is the way we've got to go. Jesus invokes a special blessing on people who realize that this is the true story. This is where and how God is at work. Those who recognize it, and are not offended because they were expecting something else, will know God's blessing.

The welcome Jesus offers for all who abandon themselves to his mercy is the welcome God offers through him. How has his welcome made a difference for you?

PRAY

When Jesus declares in the old translation that he is "meek and lowly of heart," he isn't boasting that he's attained some special level of spiritual achievement. He is encouraging us to believe that he isn't going to stand over us a like a policeman, isn't going to be cross with us like an angry schoolteacher. This is the invitation which pulls back the curtain and lets us see who "the father" really is—and encourages us to come into his loving, welcoming presence.

Reread verses 28-30 and bring your struggles and burdens to Jesus. Accept his yoke and the rest he offers.

THE KING IS ACCUSED

Matthew 12:1-50

Jesus is surrounded by pressures on all sides. His own followers don't yet really understand what he is doing. People are badgering him from every direction to heal them, to cast out evil spirits, to be there for them in their every need. At the same time, opposition is growing. Herod is not far away. Religious pressure groups are stirring up trouble. Some are even saying he's in league with the devil. He knows where it's all leading. And still he goes on.

OPEN

How do you respond to pressure from such things as workload or criticism?

STUDY

1. *Read Matthew 12:1-50.* What two challenges regarding the sabbath does Jesus face in 12:1-14 and how does he respond?

2. Jesus wasn't saying the sabbath was a bad idea, or that God had changed his mind. The sabbath laws were meant to ensure that God's love for his people would not be interrupted by people's over-eagerness to work more than they should. Jesus was attacking the way it had become so powerful a system that people who agitated for strict sabbath observance had forgotten whose law it was or what such laws were supposed to be all about—God's love for his people.

What are examples in church of things or rules seeming to matter more than people?

3. How does Jesus communicate to the Pharisees that not only do people matter more than things but also that he matters more than the temple and their system of laws?

4. The temple was the supreme physical symbol of Jewish identity. Why do Jesus' words and actions provoke such a violent response in the Pharisees that they plot to get rid of him (v. 14)?

5. In 12:15-21, Matthew quotes from Isaiah 42 which speaks of a mysterious figure whom God calls "my servant." This person will bring God's blessing and justice to the world. How is the servant to accomplish his task?

6. Matthew sees Jesus as the servant of Isaiah 42, not only when he would die a cruel death, but also in the style of what he was already

doing in Galilee. He was going about bringing God's restoration wherever it was needed, not by making a fuss but by gently leading people into God's healing love.

If the world will hope in the servant (v. 21), then hard-worked and hard-pressed church workers—and all who come to the Bible and who come to Jesus looking for help—can find fresh hope in him. How can the servant be a model and guide for us as we face various pressures?

7. Why would Jesus' opponents conclude that he must be in league with the prince of demons (12:22-32)?

8. How does Jesus counter the charge that he is in league with demonic forces?

The healings Jesus was doing were not the sort of thing you could achieve by brilliant artistry and technology like an architect. Nor was it a matter of practicing for long hard hours like a musician. His opponents accused him of deriving his powers from the prince of demons. The alternative would mean that he was acting in the power and spirit of Israel's God. And if that was the case, it would vindicate everything else Jesus was saying and doing.

9. Look at Matthew 12:33-42. Jesus' opponents ask him for a clue so they can know the truth of what's going on. He refuses to provide one except for his coming burial and resurrection. He accuses them of not being able to spot the clues because they are too busy with their own agendas.

How were the people of Nineveh (Jonah 3:1-10) and the queen of the south or Sheba (1 Kings 10:1-13) different from Jesus' opponents?

10. How can our agendas or priorities cloud us to what God might be saying to us?

11. In the two hundred years before Christ there were various attempts to bring about revival and renewal in Judaism. None of the reformations made a lasting difference. Israel remained sinful and compromised. How does this historical context shed light on Matthew 12:43-45?

12. In 12:46-50 how does Jesus identify his true family?

The point Jesus made is not so much a negative one about his physical family as a strong and positive one about his disciples. For much of this chapter, Jesus has been assailed and attacked by people who regard him as dangerous, subversive and possibly demonic. But here are some people sitting around him who are doing God's will by listening to his kingdom teaching. They are his true family.

13. What have been the rewards for you of being part of Jesus' family?

PRAY

In this Scripture passage you have seen people who accused Jesus and found fault with what he did and how he did it. You have also seen people who listened in humility and acted in obedience. Pray that you will not find fault with what he does, but will listen and obey so that you live as a full member of his family.

NOTE ON MATTHEW 12:31-32

The warning in verses 31-32 has often worried devout readers. If you are worried about committing this sin, it's a good sign that you haven't! Still it remains serious in terms of the decision we reach about Jesus. He warns against looking at the work of the Spirit and declaring that it must be the devil's doing. If you do that, it's not just that you *won't* be forgiven; you *can't* be forgiven, because you have cut off the very channel along which forgiveness would come. Once you declare that the only remaining bottle of water is poisoned, you condemn yourself to dying of thirst.

Sowing and Harvesting

Matthew 13:1-53

Matthew, in collecting together the parables which form this long chapter, has put them more or less at the center of his whole Gospel. Chapter 13 is the third of the five "discourses" which punctuate his book (Matthew 5—7; 10; 13; 18; and 23—25). These stories draw together all that has been going on so far in the Gospel and point ahead to what is still to come. In particular, several of the parables look ahead to the warning of a great coming judgment in which God will establish the kingdom once and for all by rooting out all wickedness.

Sometimes we ask, Why doesn't God step in and stop the tragedies, the accidents, the tyrants and bullies who force their own plans on people and crush opposition. Why is God apparently silent? Jesus' parables are not a direct answer to the question; probably no direct answer can be given in this life. But they show through various stories that God's sovereign rule over the world isn't such a straightforward thing as people imagine. Would people really like it if God were to rule the world directly and immediately so that our every thought and action were weighed, instantly judged and if necessary punished, in the scales of his absolute holiness?

OPEN

When have you looked at a situation and asked, "Why doesn't God *do* something?" If you received what seemed to be an answer, what was it?

STUDY

1. *Read Matthew 13:1-23.* What makes the difference in the outcome of the four plantings of seeds?

2. Jesus' hearers believed that God was beginning his work of rescuing them from their enemies. Like a farmer starting a new agricultural year, God would sow his field with crops that would bring in a harvest. How is the parable a retelling of Jesus' own ministry?

3. In Matthew 13:10 the disciples asked, "Why are you speaking to them in parables?" Jesus' quotation in Matthew 13:14-15 from Isaiah 6:9-10 has troubled readers for centuries. Is God's intention that people not hear and understand so he can judge them? Did Jesus tell parables *so that* people would not understand, because if they did they'd be saved—something he *didn't* want to happen? Jesus knew danger was mounting against him from Jewish leaders and Roman authorities because of his subversive announcement of the kingdom. He knew therefore that being indirect (so that those on the outside would in fact not really understand what he was saying so his danger wouldn't increase too quickly) was the only safe course. Only those on the inside, his loyal followers, must be allowed to glimpse what Jesus was really teaching. These stories buy Jesus time. There would come a time for more open revelation (Matthew 10:26-27).[1]

---

[1]See N. T. Wright, *Jesus and the Victory of God* (Minneapolis: Fortress, 1996), pp. 236-39, esp. p. 237.

When Jesus said "If you've got ears, then listen!" (v. 9) it should alert us to the fact that he meant "I know this isn't obvious; you're going to have to think about it!" Jesus wanted them to struggle with what he was saying, to talk about it among themselves, to think it through. What teachings of Jesus have you struggled with and why?

4. What might make us spiritually blind and deaf to what God is doing in the world today?

5. The interpretation of the parable of the sower in Matthew 13:18-23 is both very specific to Jesus' own context and very relevant to Christian preaching in our own day. Which of the four reactions to the word most closely indicates where you are?

6. Jesus says that care and thought are needed in the task of hearing the word of the kingdom. Stones may need moving. Thorns may need uprooting. If you are not where you want to be, and where God wants you, in the parable, what steps might be needed?

Again and again in Jewish thought we find the belief that God must delay his final action in order to give people time to repent. As Isaiah saw, the word goes out and does its own work in people's hearts and lives. The way to bear fruit is by hearing *and understanding.* This takes time and sometimes hard work.

7. *Read Matthew 13:24-43.* How do you see the theme of waiting in these parables?

8. Waiting is what we all find difficult. Jesus' followers weren't interested in God's timetable. They had one of their own and they expected God to conform to it. Saying that God is delaying his final judgment can look like saying that God is inactive or uncaring. But when we look at Jesus' own public career, we see one who was very active, deeply compassionate, battling with evil and defeating it—and still warning that the final overthrow of the enemy was yet to come. We who live after Calvary and Easter know that God did indeed act suddenly and dramatically at that moment.

How can knowing that God acted suddenly and dramatically in the cross and resurrection help us to wait patiently for God to act in the world or in our lives?

9. How will God's justice and God's mercy be shown at the close of the age (vv. 36-43)?

God is not a sadistic monster who would happily consign most of his beloved, image-bearing creatures to eternal fire. But neither is God an indulgent grandparent determined to spoil the youngsters rotten by letting them do whatever they like. Jesus was warning his listeners that, though what they were hoping for would indeed come soon, God's judgment might not be as straightforward as they thought.

10. Thinking of what the sun is like in the Middle East, what do you envision when you read the words "the righteous will shine like the sun in the kingdom of their father"?

i

It's clear that Jesus is talking about a redeemed, renewed people that is at last what God meant it to be: the mirror in which the rest of creation can see who its Creator really is and can worship and serve him truly. The same mirror in which the world can see the true God will reveal that this God is supremely loving, wise, beautiful, holy, just and true. When we read the awesome judgment scenes in the Bible, it is that combination of attributes we must learn to see.

11. Jesus and his kingdom message are meant to startle us. Part of the really shocking thing is that they are the true fulfillment of the long story of God and Israel, and indeed of God and the world. *Read Matthew 13:44-53*. What decisions are made in these parables?

12. How do these parables encourage action?

The world isn't simply going round and round in circles as many religions and philosophies teach. It's going in a straight line toward a goal, and it's going there quite fast. The coming of Jesus began the process of final judgment. As he taught and lived the kingdom, the world was divided sharply in two, into those who were swept off their feet by him and those who resisted and rejected his gospel.

13. Looking over Matthew 13, what basic truths about the kingdom stand out to you?

PRAY

Pray that you will have ears to hear and understand what God is saying to you.

THE HOMETOWN PROPHET

Matthew 13:54—14:36

Perhaps it requires a particular kind of humility to hear something new and disturbing from someone very familiar. Certainly it required something the people of Nazareth didn't have. Jesus came to his own people and his own people did not receive him well. *He's just the boy from down the street,* they said. *He's just a local lad. Here are his brothers and sisters still living with us. He can't be anyone special.* Jesus' teaching was shocking, explosive and dangerous. Sensible people would be worried about it. Those who had known him from boyhood would be tempted to doubt whether he could possibly be serious.

OPEN

When have you said something that was true but that was not appreciated or accepted? Looking back, do you wish you had done anything differently? Why or why not?

STUDY

1. *Read Matthew 13:54—14:12.* How does Jesus violate expectations in his hometown?

2. This account of John the Baptist comes right after a long series of parables Jesus told of the kingdom. How does this incident indicate that Jesus' teaching was more than harmless, simple lessons about life, morality or spirituality?

Just because people are offended by what you say, that doesn't mean you are a heaven-sent prophet. But equally, if the signs that God is at work are present elsewhere—as they were abundantly in Jesus' case—then rejection should never be taken as an indication that you are off track or that God has withdrawn his blessing. If new creation and new life are going forward, those who are invested heavily in the old creation and the old ways of life are bound to be offended.

3. John the Baptist cleared the path for Jesus by warning people of the coming kingdom and preparing them for the coming king. He made it clear that Herod could not be the true king of the Jews; his moral life was such a mess that the idea was unthinkable.

As you read this story how do you react to each of the characters?

4. What weaknesses in Herod prompt him to carry out this series of events?

5. What Herod-like characteristic might be lurking in your own life, even in small ways?

6. Why did Matthew put the story of the death of John the Baptist side by side with the story of Jesus visiting his hometown?

7. How might we be called to stand against what is evil, and what reactions might we receive for doing so?

8. When Jesus learned of John's death he slipped away to be quiet and alone, but the crowds discovered him and thronged all around him.

   Read Matthew 14:13-36. Under the circumstances in Matthew 14:13-14, what is remarkable about Jesus' reaction to the crowds?

9. The disciples observe Jesus' compassion and come to him with a suggestion which seems best for the crowds and for him. Why do you think Jesus counters with "You give them something to eat"?

10. In the face of the crowd's hunger, the disciples said, "All we have here is five loaves of bread and two fish." Think of a problem or need that stirs your compassion but that appears too huge for you to do anything about. How would you complete this statement? "All I have here is . . ."

What Jesus does with what we give him is so mysterious and powerful that it's hard to describe in words. We blunder in with our ideas. We offer, uncomprehending, what little we have. Jesus takes ideas, loaves and fishes, money, a sense of humor, time, energy, talents, love, artistic gifts, skill with words, quickness of eye or fingers, whatever we have to offer. He holds them before his Father with prayer and blessing. Then, breaking them (there's the cost, yet again) so they are ready for use, he gives them back to us to give to those who need them.

11. Jesus sent the disciples off in the boat while he dismissed the crowds (14:22). Although the disciples had seen Jesus' power, heard his teaching and prayed his prayer, suddenly they were stuck. Experienced fishermen, they were struggling with the oars, unable to make headway against the wind.

Then there is Peter, who, caught between glory and terror, walks on the water toward Jesus, looks around at the storm and starts to sink. In a way it is encouraging because it rings so true in our Christian experience. The moment when we are most strongly tempted to give up is probably the moment when, if only we knew it, help is just a step away. This story can be read as a picture of the life of faith, or rather the life of half-faith, faith mixed with fear and doubt, which is the typical state of so many Christians, as it was with the disciples.

When have you moved ahead with half-faith, and what was the result?

12. Consider some practical ways that you can keep your focus on Christ and not get caught up in the surrounding storm. Which idea(s) will you put into effect this week?

PRAY

Bring your fears, even your sense of panic, to the Lord and call out like Peter, "Master, rescue me!" Thank him that he has never failed you and will not fail you.

Pray also about others' needs which appear overwhelming. Bring what you have to Jesus, no matter how inadequate it looks, and allow him to use it as he wishes.

PURE THROUGH AND THROUGH

Matthew 15:1-39

The story is told of an archbishop visiting a local church and meeting a man who had been going there for fifty years. "You must have seen many changes in that time," said the archbishop.

"Yes," replied the man, "and I opposed them all."

Some people like to do things in church the same way year after year. Some people like to do things as differently as they can as often as they can. Novelty for the sake of novelty is just as sterile as custom for the sake of custom. Such personal preferences make a poor basis for wise judgment and decisions.

OPEN

How do you distinguish between a church tradition or innovation that is healthy and one that is not?

STUDY

1. *Read Matthew 15:1-20.* How does Jesus turn the tables on the Pharisees with his response to their challenge?

In the Ten Commandments the Israelites were commanded to honor their parents, which included looking after them in their old age. In the Pharisees' traditions it was permitted for someone to make a gift to the temple of an equivalent amount to what they might have spent on their parents. If they did that, they were deemed to be under no further obligation. This had an obvious benefit to the temple, and indeed might give the appearance of great piety. But it undermined the whole point of the law.

2. Jesus wasn't just saying, "If in doubt, go for innovation!" What instead was Jesus' point about how to judge any particular tradition or innovation in church?

3. How does "what comes out of the mouth" (v. 11) reveal what is in the heart?

4. Why is it easier to keep oneself pure externally than to keep oneself pure internally?

Long before psychologists noticed that what people say is an indication of what's really going on inside their thoughts and imaginations, particularly when they're not concentrating very hard, Jesus made the same point. The motivations which point toward actions give themselves away in thoughts and words which come bubbling up from the depths of the personality, showing that, whatever outward purity codes the person may keep, the innermost self of that person needs to be changed if they are to be what God intends and wants.

In this passage Jesus does not offer the remedy for the condition he has diagnosed. Ultimately he himself is the remedy, as in his death and resurrection and gift of the Spirit he deals with the wickedness and uncleanness that infects the human race. The remedy needs to be applied to the disease deep down inside the human personality so that when we stand before God he will see us, as he always intended, pure through and through.

5. *Read Matthew 15:21-39.* What is startling or puzzling about what happens in the encounter Jesus has with the Canaanite woman?

6. How does the Canaanite woman demonstrate her persistence?

7. What is Jesus' basis for at first refusing to help?

8. Why does he then agree to help?

9. What does this episode add to the discussion in this chapter of the themes of clean and unclean, pure and unpure?

10. Matthew includes a second story about Jesus feeding thousands of people in the wilderness (vv. 29-39) quite soon after a very similar story in chapter 14.

How is this event similar to, and different from, the feeding of the five thousand in Matthew 14:13-22?

11. Matthew is underlining his belief that the long-awaited time is now at last coming to pass. The healings are not just signs of special power. They are signs of the fact that Jesus is fulfilling the old prophecies. Here, finally, is what Israel had been waiting for all along. No wonder the crowd "gave praise to the God of Israel."

What work of mercy or issues that cannot wait may God be asking you, your fellowship or your church to take on?

PRAY

The Canaanite woman showed the same remarkable faith of the Gentile centurion mentioned in Matthew 8:10. She brought her requests with faith and persistence. She was not content to wait for the promises that might be fulfilled in the distant future. Bring your desires and requests to Jesus and pray as humbly but as boldly as she did.

NOTE ON MATTHEW 15:21-28

The story of the Canaanite woman raises several knotty questions. First, why does Jesus seem to suggest that he came exclusively for Israel and not everyone? God's people, Israel, needed to know that their God was now at last fulfilling his promises. If God's new life was to come to the world, it would come through Israel. That's why Israel had to hear the message first. But if Israel is indeed the promise-bearing people, then Israel's Messiah will ultimately bring blessing to the whole world. The Canaanite woman in fact reminds Jesus of this by saying that even so-called dogs will share the scraps that fall from the children's table. In this way her remarkable faith is honored as was that of another Gentile (Matthew 8:10), the like of which Jesus hadn't even seen in Israel. The woman's faith broke through the waiting period, and Jesus congratulated her for her great faith.

Perhaps an even more troublesome issue is that Jesus seems to imply that the woman and Gentiles in general are "dogs" (v. 26). This is regularly made the basis of a fashionable theory concerning Jesus' innate prejudices. This is not the only way to read the story, as Caird and Hurst's *New Testament Theology* (p. 395) makes clear:

> Apart from the obvious danger of building an entire reconstruction on one reported incident, one must be especially aware of the problem incurred by the loss of *tone* in any reported saying of Jesus. . . . Jesus' words, which in cold print seem so austere, were almost certainly spoken with a smile and a tone of voice which invited the woman's witty reply. Jesus must have been aware of the prejudice against Gentiles which existed among many of his contemporaries, and in view of the use of irony found elsewhere in his teaching, it would be surprising not to find a vestige of it in this.

Bailey in *Jesus Through Middle Eastern Eyes* (pp. 223ff.) suggests that Jesus takes the narrow-minded attitudes of his disciples and presses them to their logical extreme. As Bailey says, "The verbalization is authentic to their [the disciples'] attitudes and feelings, but shocking when put into words and thrown in the face of a desperate, kneeling woman pleading for the sanity of her daughter. It is acutely embarrassing to hear and see one's deepest prejudices verbalized and demonstrated." Jesus ultimately not only honors the woman as one of the few who "bests" him in an argument but also teaches his disciples a lesson regarding their mistaken ideas about the kingdom.

SIGNS OF THE TIMES

Matthew 16:1-28

Drive along a city street, especially at night, and your eyes will be dazzled with signs of all sorts. Some of them are necessary to tell you where to go and where not to go; others are merely for decoration and information. Many others are designed to catch your imagination—and your money. Part of growing up is learning to distinguish signs that matter, which must be obeyed, from signs that don't matter, that can (and perhaps should) be ignored.

Jesus sometimes did things which he spoke of as *signs*. Some of his powerful deeds, especially his healings, were seen as signs of who he is, signs that the disciples and probably others as well were meant to notice, to read and to understand.

OPEN

When you see or hear the phrase "signs of the times," what do you think of? How important is it to interpret the signs of the times? How difficult is it?

STUDY

1. *Read Matthew 16:1-28.* How does Jesus explain his response to the

demand of the Pharisees and Sadducees for a sign?

2. The "sign of Jonah" (v. 4) was previously explained by Jesus in Matthew 12:38-42 as pointing to his burial and resurrection. What are the true signs of God's work in our midst?

3. How can we learn to tell the difference, in our moral and spiritual life together, between the signs we must observe and those we would do better to ignore?

4. At Passover all leaven (yeast) had to be cleared out of the house, commemorating the time when the children of Israel left Egypt in such a hurry that they didn't have time to bake leavened bread. Gradually, leaven became a symbol not for something that makes bread more palatable but for something that makes bread less pure. Warning against the "leaven" of someone's teaching meant warning against ways in which the true message of God's kingdom could be corrupted, diluted or (as we say, referring to drink rather than bread), watered down.

Jesus refused to offer signs to impress the public or engage in self-aggrandizement. How should we evaluate leaders and teachers, official and unofficial, on these criteria?

5. The disciples seem dense about Jesus' meaning regarding the yeast of the Pharisees. When have you realized that God was trying to say

something to you, but it took you a while to understand?

6. When Jesus asked the disciples who people thought he was, the disciples didn't say a cozy, comforting friend of children or a "gentle Jesus, meek and mild." They compared him to prophets of the past. What were they like?

7. Many Jews of Jesus' day believed that God would send an anointed king who would spearhead the movement to free Israel from oppression and bring justice and peace to the world at last. Many believed he would be a true descendant of King David. The word for "anointed king" in the Jewish languages, Hebrew and Aramaic, is the word we normally pronounce as "Messiah."

   In the first century there were several would-be Messiahs who came and went, attracting followers who were quickly dispersed when their leader was caught by the authorities. One thing was certain. To be known as a would-be Messiah was to attract attention from the authorities, and almost certainly hostility. Thus Jesus' warning to be quiet about all this.

   How would you describe the contrast between the way of the Messiah as envisioned by Jesus and as envisioned by Peter (and presumably the other disciples) (vv. 21-28)?

8. This passage contains a dire warning for all those called to any office or vocation in God's church: the one to whom some of the greatest promises and commissions were made is the one who earned the sharpest rebuke.

What warning does Jesus' rebuke of Peter hold for those who are called to leadership in the church?

9. The disciples held to the popular idea of how God's kingdom would come. Jesus' proposal is a mirror image of that idea. The way to the kingdom is by the exact opposite road to the one the disciples—especially Peter—had in mind. Jesus insists that God thinks differently from how we mortals think. God sees everything inside out; or perhaps we should say, God sees everything the right way, whereas we see everything inside out.

When you read verses 24-26 how do you feel challenged, and how do you feel reassured?

10. In every generation there are, it seems, a few people who are prepared to take Jesus seriously, at his word in Matthew 16:24-28. What would it be like to be one of them?

PRAY

It is tempting to see the kingdom of God as one of power, where God's people rule and implement God's ways. Jesus saw the kingdom coming, however, through sacrifice and suffering. Pray that God will show you and your community how you can emulate the Messiah as we seek his will to be done on earth as it is in heaven.

NOTE ON MATTHEW 16:14

Jesus modeled his ministry not on one person alone but on a range of

Old Testament prophets. Elijah seems to be one of his primary models. He healed like Elijah did in 1 Kings 17:17-24 and 2 Kings 4:32-37. He also announced to the faithless nation that their God will come to them in anger, just as Elijah stood alone against the prophets of Baal and against the wickedness of King Ahab (1 Kings 18:16-40).

Both Jesus and Jeremiah predicted the destruction of the temple (see Jeremiah 26:1-16). Like Jeremiah, Jesus constantly ran the risk of being called a traitor to Israel's national aspirations while claiming all the time he is the true spokesman for the covenant God.[1]

NOTE ON MATTHEW 16:16

The phrase "Son of God" did not mean "the second person of the Trinity." No one at the time of Jesus thought yet that the coming king would himself be divine—though some of the things Jesus was doing and saying must already have made the disciples very puzzled, eventually coming to believe that he had all along been even more intimately associated with Israel's one God than they had ever imagined. But here the phrase "Son of God" was a biblical phrase, indicating that the king stood in a particular relation to God, adopted to be his special representative (see, for instance, 2 Samuel 7:14 and Psalm 2:7).

NOTE ON MATTHEW 16:28

The phrases about "the son of man coming in his kingdom" (v. 20) and the like are not about what we call the "second coming" of Jesus. They are about his vindication, following his suffering. They are fulfilled when he rises from the dead and is granted "all authority in heaven and on earth" (Matthew 28:18).

---

[1]See N. T. Wright, *Jesus and the Victory of God* (Minneapolis: Fortress, 1996), pp. 162-71.

FAITH AND PRAYER

Matthew 17:1-27

Mount Tabor is a large, round hill in central Galilee, the traditional site of the transfiguration, the extraordinary incident described in Matthew 17. When you go there today with a party of pilgrims, you have to get out of your bus and take a taxi to the top. They say that God is especially pleased with the Mount Tabor taxi drivers, because more praying goes on in the few minutes hurtling up or down the narrow mountain road in those cars than in the rest of the day, or possibly the week. I've heard that said of other places too, but at Mount Tabor it's especially believable.

OPEN

When have you had fruitful experiences of prayer and when have you had frustrating ones?

STUDY

1. *Read Matthew 17:1-27.* Imagine that you are there on the mountaintop as a witness to this extraordinary event described in Matthew 17:1-8. How do you react? What questions fill your mind?

2. If we are surprised and startled by this episode, we are in good company with Peter who (possibly in shock) blurts out an outlandish suggestion about building three shelters for the three shining figures. Moses (who brought the law to Israel from Mt. Sinai) and Elijah (one of the great prophets of Israel who also met God on Mt. Sinai) together represent the law and the prophets, a kind of shorthand for the whole of the Old Testament that Jews of that day would have recognized. Here Moses and Elijah seem to testify that Jesus, in the center, is the fulfillment of all of Scripture.

The scene at the transfiguration, as it is normally called, offers a strange parallel and contrast to the crucifixion (Matthew 27:33-54). What similarities and differences do you see?

3. How do these two events—the one on a mountaintop and the one on a hilltop—explain each other and help us to understand them both?

4. Having just seen Elijah on the mountaintop, the disciples are reminded that the prophet Malachi (in 4:5) declared that Elijah would return to prepare the people for the Day of the Lord. The teachers concluded that after Elijah, then the Messiah would come to take up the work from there (Matthew 17:9-13).

How does Jesus see in John the Baptist the fulfillment of the promise that Elijah will (and has) come?

5. The disciples didn't recognize John as fulfilling the role of Elijah, because John didn't do what they expected, blasting everyone into

shape with celestial thunderbolts. Only looking back did they now see it clearly. When did you only discover what God was doing in and through you when you looked back?

6. What are the various frustrations of the people in Matthew 17:14-21?

7. When Moses came down from Mt. Sinai, he found the people had broken the law by making a golden calf; and he was naturally very angry. The disciples haven't exactly been rebellious, but Jesus is nonetheless angry. Why should they have had faith by now?

8. What have you been given or what experiences have you had that should have instilled a deeper faith than you have now?

9. In Matthew 13:31-32 Jesus noted that mustard seeds are tiny but productive. What he said about the kingdom then he now says about individual faith. How are the kingdom and faith connected?

10. With Jesus gone for a day or two up the mountain, the disciples were faced with a new challenge, and they couldn't do anything about it. Maybe they thought they had the power in themselves. Maybe they thought they could do it without bothering God too much. The severity of the problem is matched by Jesus' amazing promise. The

size of your faith isn't important; what's important is the God in whom you believe. The smallest prayer to the one true God will produce great things; the most elaborate devotions to a "god" of your own making, or someone else's, will be useless or worse.

Jesus had instructed the Twelve to be "as shrewd as snakes, and as innocent as doves" (Matthew 10:16). How does he put his own advice into practice in the event described in Matthew 17:24-27?

11. Every Jew all over the world was supposed to pay a small sum each year (a *didrachma*, a little coin) to help support the temple in Jerusalem. Jesus did not believe that the temple tax was proper. But he was also a master strategist. Now was not the time, Galilee was not the place, and a minor tax collector not the person for Jesus' major protest to be made. Before too long he would be in the temple itself, turning over tables, spilling coins right and left (Mattthew 21:12). For the moment it was better not to raise the alarm and not to let word get out that his kingdom movement was indeed aimed at challenging the authority of the temple and its rulers. So the tax had better be paid.

What difficult situations do you find yourself in that call for Jesus' wisdom and strategy?

PRAY

If you believed Jesus' words about faith 100 percent, what would you pray for? Pray in that way. Consider a time of fasting in connection with your prayer.

16

HUMILITY IN THE KINGDOM

Matthew 18:1-35

Following Jesus means learning to look at life, at the world, at God, at yourself, through the other end of the telescope. We all find it difficult (particularly a group of youngish men like Jesus' disciples) to think that weakness and vulnerability are anything other than things to be ashamed of. But humility is what counts in God's kingdom, because pride and arrogance are the things which, more than anything else in God's world, distort and ultimately destroy human lives—their own and those of people they affect.

OPEN

What kinds of people are considered important in the church and why?

STUDY

1. *Read Matthew 18:1-14.* Which of Jesus' statements strikes you as the most extreme and why?

2. Jesus gives far sterner warnings here than anything he ever says about the "big" sins such as murder, adultery and theft. What do his strong words say about what God values most?

3. Who are the "little ones" in society—those who have the least power and are most vulnerable?

The weakest, least significant human being you can think of is the clearest possible signpost to what the kingdom of God will be like. God's kingdom—the future time when heaven rules on earth—won't be about the survival of the fittest. It won't be the result of some long evolutionary process in which the strongest, the fastest, the loudest, the angriest people get to the front ahead of everybody else. Jesus tosses all that out of the window and instead calls out a little child: shy, vulnerable, unsure of herself, but trusting and with clear eyes, ready to listen, to be loved and to love, to learn and to grow. This is what true greatness is like, he says. Go and learn about it. In particular, go and imitate it.

4. *Read Matthew 18:15-35.* What are the steps toward reconciliation that Jesus spells out here?

5. When you have been sinned against, what is the difference between saying, "It didn't really matter," and genuine reconciliation?

6. When have you seen or felt reconciliation create a closer bond between people?

7. When I have been involved in difficult discussions within a family or a Christian fellowship, this is the Scripture passage I've always tried to bear in mind. It is severely practical as well as ruthlessly idealistic: not a bad combination. Many Christians have taken the paper-over-the-cracks option, believing that "forgiveness" means pretending that everything is all right, that the other person hasn't really done anything wrong. That simply won't do. Forgiveness is when it *did* happen, and it *did* matter, and you're going to deal with it and end up loving and accepting one another again anyway. Reconciliation can come only after the problem has been faced.

   In response to Peter's question in verse 21, Jesus answers with a parable. In your own words what do you think is the central meaning of this parable?

8. Why is forgiving so difficult?

9. In what situations are you most likely to demand "payment" from others as the servant did in verses 28-30?

10. Every time you accuse someone else, you accuse yourself. Every time you forgive someone else, you pass on a drop of water out of the bucketful that God has already given you. To put it another way, forgive-

ness is like the air in your lungs. There's only room for you to inhale the next lungful when you've just breathed out the previous one. Whatever the spiritual, moral and emotional equivalent of the lungs may be, it's either open or closed. If it's open, able and willing to forgive others, it will also be open to receive God's love and forgiveness. But if it's locked up to the one, it will be locked up to the other.

With whom do you need to seek reconciliation? What is the next step you should take?

PRAY

Pray for the "little ones" in your society, those who are most vulnerable. Ask God to show you what you can do to speak up for them, protect them and empower them.

Pray also that you will forgive as you have been forgiven. Pray for guidance about steps you should take toward reconciliation where necessary.

NOTE ON MATTHEW 18:6-9

Jesus didn't mean us literally to cut off hands and feet and pluck out eyes. That kind of self-mutilation is a sign of mental disorder, not of genuine holiness. It's like the two-ton millstone round the neck: a huge, typically Middle Eastern exaggeration to make the point. But the point is no less serious for that. Anyone who has ever tried to break a bad moral habit will know that it sometimes feels like cutting off a hand or foot. And the habits and attitudes that Jesus has in his sights in this passage are as hard as any. Cutting off the "hand" that refuses to give to the poor; cutting off the "foot" that refuses to walk to the soup kitchen to help out; and in particular, plucking out the "eye" that refuses to notice the weak, the vulnerable, the helpless all around us, in our cities, on our streets, in our wider world: all these pose a challenge every bit as severe as the day Jesus first issued it.

17

POSSIBLE WITH GOD

Matthew 19:1—20:16

We live at a time when what used to be thought of as Christian behavior in the area of marriage and family has been rejected by large swathes of Western society, though upheld in many traditional cultures, including several explicitly non-Christian ones. The rampant individualism of the last few hundred years in the West has left families and children in bad shape, as people act on the belief that they have, as individuals, a "right to happiness" which overrides all considerations of loyalty, keeping vows and the duty to bring up lovingly the children one has brought into the world.

Nobody, certainly not Jesus, ever said that following him and finding God's kingdom-way in these matters would be easy. But nobody should imagine that it's just an optional extra. As Jesus comes closer to Jerusalem and to his own astonishing act of self-denial and self-sacrifice, we should take note that the call to follow him extends to the most personal and intimate details of our lives.

OPEN

When have you found satisfaction in keeping a promise? How have you benefited from other people keeping their promises?

STUDY

1. *Read Matthew 19:1-15.* What main points about marriage and family does Jesus make?

2. In 1 Corinthians 7:15, Paul allows a further ground of divorce: if an unbelieving partner desires to separate from a Christian believer, the believer should not ultimately refuse. But in both cases it is quite clear that the Christian norm is lifelong marriage. God is in the business of making people new from the inside. But it's not automatic. Just because you have signed on as a follower of Jesus, that doesn't mean you won't be tempted to do many wrong things. In fact, it means that temptation levels will almost certainly increase. The way this newness works must be through your own decisions, your own thinking things through, your own willpower aided and strengthened at every point by the Holy Spirit.

   How do both the Pharisees and the disciples misunderstand the heart of God?

3. In what ways are children "the sort the kingdom of heaven belongs to" (19:14)?

4. The renewal of life God offers, in the sphere of marriage as everywhere else, will come through the willing, intelligent obedience of wholehearted women and men who think out what it means to be loyal to God and to other people, especially to their marriage partner, and who take steps to put it into practice.

There weren't very many rich people in Jesus' world, and such as there were would be figures of note. *Read Matthew 19:16-22*. The wealthy young man has a worthy aim: to "possess the life of the age to come" when God's sovereign, saving rule would transform everything. Despite his moral life, what is still lacking?

5. If salvation is not achieved by giving away possessions, why do you think Jesus gives the young man the instructions in 19:21?

6. *Read Matthew 19:23-30*. What assumptions lie behind the disciples' astonishment in 19:25?

7. When have you asked the Lord, either silently or out loud, the question Peter asks in 19:27 (or one similar to it)?

8. Jesus' point about those at the front and back in our society is similar to what he said about the "little ones" in Matthew 18:1-14. There is a great reversal in God's kingdom. Why does this seem so impossible to us now?

9. As we have seen in this chapter and the previous ones, Jesus often exaggerates hugely to make his point. The point of verse 24 is that it's unthinkable. That is the moment when all human calculations and possibilities stop and God's new possibilities start. What

is impossible in human terms, Jesus' followers are to discover to their amazement, is possible to God (19:26). God's new world comes through the complete reversal of all normal ideas of kingship and earthly greatness.

The disciples could have assumed that because they had been so close to Jesus, they would be the favored few for all time. People who work in church circles can easily assume that they are the special ones, God's inner circle. *Read Matthew 20:1-16.* How is Jesus' parable a natural extension of 19:30?

10. What is Jesus saying about God and humanity?

11. Consider what Matthew 19:1—20:16 has said to you about the priorities of God and how they are a reversal of the world's values. How could your fellowship encourage faithful marriages, welcome the least in society or encourage an appropriate view of possessions?

PRAY

Which part of today's Scripture has touched you most deeply? How is the Holy Spirit speaking to you about changes you need to make? Pray about those issues. Thank God for his generous grace.

NOTE ON MATTHEW 19:21

Is Jesus' command to the young man to give everything away a universal instruction? The young man seems to want to collect commandments he's kept, like one might collect coins or butterflies. All right, Jesus says, this is the one that will complete your collection: give everything away! In order to be complete, you must be empty. In order to have everything, you must have nothing. In order to be fully signed up to God's service, you must be signed off from everything else. As with the previous comments about celibacy (19:11-12), this commandment was not given to everybody. Jesus did not often tell people to give away everything and follow him. When he did, it was either because, as in the case of the Twelve, he wanted them to be free so that they could be with him all the time and share his work; or because, as with this young man, he sensed that his possessions had become his idol that would eventually kill him unless he renounced it.

THE ARRIVAL OF THE KING

Matthew 20:17—21:32

Young politicians try to guess who's going to be powerful. They attach themselves to him or her, so that if they've guessed right they will be rewarded handsomely for their early allegiance. People play games like that all the time. It produces cheap "loyalty" that's not worth a thing, hollow "friendships" that don't go deeper than the outward smile, and easy betrayals when things go wrong.

The disciples had attached themselves to Jesus, the Messiah, the coming king who was on his way to Jerusalem. Throughout these chapters of Matthew is the head-on clash between what Jesus is trying to explain to the disciples and what they assume their journey to Jerusalem is all about. They are so convinced that he must be following the sort of plan they have in mind that they simply can't register his repeated warnings that it's all going to be very different.

OPEN

Suppose today Jesus asked you, "What do you want me to do for you?" How would you answer?

STUDY

1. *Read Matthew 20:17-34.* How do you explain the gulf between Jesus' prediction of what will happen to him and the request James and John make through their mother?

2. How are pagan rulers and Christians to contrast with one another (20:24-28)?

3. A "ransom" in the disciples' world is what someone might pay to give freedom to a slave. Jesus saw his approaching fate as the payment that would set free those who were enslaved in sin and wickedness, not least those who were in the grips of the lust for power and position—yes, people like James and John.

   In Matthew 20:21 and 32 Jesus asks what a pair of brothers want and what a pair of blind men want. How do these pairs and their requests compare and contrast?

4. For James and John in the previous passage, the thought that Jesus was going to be king meant that perhaps they would get to sit on either side of him. What would two blind beggars outside Jericho typically be asking for?

5. Why would Jesus' actions and question startle the blind men (20:32)?

The two men have left one life behind and have begun a new one. It can happen to anyone who asks Jesus for something and finds Jesus' searching question coming straight back at them, piercing through the outer crust and finding the real request bubbling up underneath.

6. When has the Lord gotten to the heart of what you really wanted and then answered your prayer?

7. *Read Matthew 21:1-11.* Put yourself into this scene as one of the crowd along the roadside. What are you doing? What do you see and hear? What emotions are you feeling? What are your expectations?

8. The whole procession was saying, in a way, what James and John and their mother had been saying in their way (20:20-22). Everyone wants Jesus to ride into the city and become the sort of king they want him to be. Jesus intends to answer their prayers as he intends to answer ours. He doesn't wait for our motives to be pure; he has come to seek and rescue the lost. However, at the same time he must answer in his own way. Precisely because Jesus says "yes" to the people's desires at the deepest level, he will have to say "no" or "wait" to the desires they are conscious of and which they express.

The temple in Jerusalem, instead of being regarded as the place where Israel could come to God in prayer, had come to stand for the violent longings for a great revolution in which the kingdom of God would come by force. *Read Matthew 21:12-22.* How does Jesus demonstrate God's judgment on the temple?

9. How can a religious system get in the way of worship of the true God?

10. *Read Matthew 21:23-32.* Imagine the crowd all around, watching what could turn into a police investigation or arrest turning instead into a high-pressure and high-profile public debate, with the upstart from the country leaving the sophisticated city folk mumbling that they don't know the answer to his question. How does Jesus confound the question of the chief priests and elders?

11. If the Jewish leaders truly understood what John had been doing, they would know where Jesus got the right to behave as Messiah in the temple courts. But Jesus isn't finished. He presses home his advantage. Why does he dare to tell them that "the tax-collectors and prostitutes are going into God's kingdom ahead of you" (21:31)?

The challenge of this passage for us today is partly to make sure we are responding to Jesus, allowing him to confront us at any point where we have been like the second son and said "yes" to God while in fact going off in the other direction.

12. Where have you said "yes" to God but not followed through? How might you begin to put your "yes" into action today?

PRAY

Reread Matthew 20:25-28. Pray that God will show you any ways in which you are tempted to lord your authority over others. Ask God to give you the Christlike heart of a servant.

NOTE ON MATTHEW 21:18-22

Jesus came looking for fruit, but when he found none he solemnly declared that the tree would be barren forever. That's exactly what he was doing with the temple. And the promise to the disciples, which follows from it, is not a general comment about the power of prayer to do extraordinary things (though of course it is true that all sorts of things can be accomplished through prayer). The promise is far more focused than that. Saying to "this mountain" that it should be "lifted up and thrown into the sea," when you are standing right beside the temple mountain, was bound to be taken as another coded warning about what would happen to the temple as God's judgment fell upon his rebellious people for holding the ideology that military might and conquest would suffice.

The lines of Jesus' work through the earlier days in Galilee come together with new force. All along he'd been acting as if you could get, by coming to him, the blessings you'd normally get by going to the temple. Now he is declaring, in powerful actions, that the temple itself is under God's judgment.

PARABLES AND QUESTIONS

Matthew 21:33—22:46

The trouble with politicians today," my friend said to me the other evening, "is that they always tell us that if we vote for them things will get better. If only they'd tell us the truth—that the world is a dangerous place, that there are lots of wicked people trying to exploit each other, and that they will do their best to steer us through—then we might believe them."

The same sort of thing happens in the church as well. We want to hear a nice story about God throwing the party open to everyone. We want to be inclusive, to let everyone in. We don't want to know about judgment on the wicked or about demanding standards of holiness or about weeping and gnashing of teeth. But God wants us to be grown up, not babies, and part of being grown up is that we learn that actions have consequences and that moral choices matter. The great, deep mystery of God's forgiveness isn't the same as saying that whatever we do isn't really important because it will all work out somehow.

OPEN

In your Christian experience, do you think the judgment of God has been underemphasized, overemphasized or emphasized to about the right extent? How do you think most Christians in your society would answer that question?

STUDY

1. *Read Matthew 21:33-46.* Jesus is still talking with the chief priests and elders (21:23) and here we find that Pharisees were also in the audience (21:45). What is the message of the parable for them?

2. In Jesus' parable and in his quote from Psalm 118, how are the son and the stone both rejected and both vindicated?

Jesus, interpreting his own story, quotes from two biblical passages, Psalm 118 and Daniel 2. In the book of Daniel, the Babylonian king Nebuchadnezzar had a dream of a huge statue. Its head was made of gold, its chest and arms of silver, its middle and thighs of bronze, its legs of iron, and its feet of a mixture of iron and clay—each part of the statue representing the successive kingdoms of the world. Then there came a stone which struck the statue on its feet of iron and clay and smashed them; and the whole statue came crashing down. The stone itself became a great mountain and filled the whole earth (Daniel 2). For the Jews of Jesus' day, the kingdoms of the world, starting with Babylon and Persia, had gone on until at last it was Rome's turn. Now surely was the moment for the Stone to appear— God's Messiah.

3. *Read Matthew 22:1-14.* Why do you think this parable makes many readers uncomfortable?

4. How does the king display both lavish generosity and unyielding judgment?

5. Why do people today refuse God's invitation to the feast?

We want to hear that everyone is all right exactly as they are, that God loves us as we are and doesn't want us to change. People often say this when they want to justify particular types of behavior; but the argument doesn't work. Love wants the best for the beloved. God hates what ruthless, violent, arrogant and manipulative people are doing and the effect it has on everyone else—and on themselves too. If he is a good God, he cannot allow that sort of behavior, and that sort of person, if they don't change, to remain forever in the party he's throwing for his Son. That is the point of the end of the story.

6. *Read Matthew 22:15-33.* The issue of paying taxes to the Roman emperor who conquered much of the Middle East was one of the hottest topics in Jesus' day. Tell people they shouldn't pay, and you might end up on a cross. At the same time anyone leading a kingdom-of-God movement would be expected to oppose the tax or face the ridicule and resentment of the people.

How does Jesus turn the Pharisees' trick question back on themselves?

Jesus wasn't trying to give an answer, for all time, on the relationship between God and political authority. He was countering the Pharisees' challenge with a sharp challenge in return. It was they who were compromised by handling images (which were forbidden to Jews) with inscriptions claiming Caesar was "Son of God."

7. In Matthew 22:23-33, how is Jesus' view of resurrection different from the theoretical view posed by the Sadducees?

8. The Sadducees were missing any real engagement with the meaning of the Bible, and any real awareness of how great and powerful the Creator God is. Israel's God was and is the Creator of the world, who is content to describe himself as the God of Abraham, Isaac and Jacob even though they died long ago. He is holding them in life still, and one day they will be raised along with all God's people, past, present and future, to enjoy the new world that God will make.

Many Jewish teachers posed the question as to which was the greatest out of all the 613 commandments in the law of Moses. *Read Matthew 22:34-46.* How is love of God and others different from following laws yet still fulfilling laws?

9. What status does Jesus claim for the Messiah (and therefore for himself)?

10. After this exchange, why do you think no one dares to ask Jesus any more questions (22:46)?

11. The next occasions when Jesus will meet his opponents will be in

the garden when they arrest him, in the council when they accuse
him and on the cross when they mock him. But each time they will
know, he will know and we as Matthew's readers will know, that
he knows the answers to these questions and they do not. He also
knows, and Matthew wants us to know as well, that his arrest, trial
and crucifixion are precisely the way in which Jesus is fulfilling
the two great commandments and the way in which he is being enthroned both as David's son, the true king of Israel, and David's
master, David's Lord. Jesus knows that sin and death can only be
defeated by David's master going to meet them in single, unarmed
combat. That is why he continues his work, as Matthew will tell us,
all the way to the cross itself.

In each episode in Matthew 21:33—22:46, how does Jesus show
himself master, walking the path he chooses on his own terms?

12. Considering all of today's Scripture passage, Matthew 21:33—22:46,
    which part do you find most challenging?

PRAY

Pray that you will hear God's gracious invitation and respond daily. Pray
that you will be part of God's effort to bring in those whom the world
would consider least deserving.

WORDS OF JUDGMENT

Matthew 23:1-39

With this chapter we are launched into the last of the five great blocks of teaching which Matthew has constructed as the backbone of his Gospel. In all of this, Matthew is saying, we are to regard Jesus as being like Moses, only more so.

Moses, the Jews held, gave them the first five books of the Bible. He brought the people through the desert and led them to the point where they were ready to cross over the Jordan and go into the Promised Land. Jesus is leading his people through the desert to the point where he will lead them through death itself and on into the new world which God is going to make. Only, unlike Moses, he won't stay on this side of the river, leaving someone else to take the people across. He will go on ahead, like his namesake Joshua, and lead them himself into the new world.

OPEN

When have you been encouraged by someone going ahead of you and leading the way? Why did it make a difference?

STUDY

1. Jesus finds himself surrounded with people who are telling their

fellow Jews about the heavy packs they need to carry on their backs
for the journey, but who never dream of carrying such things themselves. *Read Matthew 23:1-22.* How are the values of Jesus different
from those of the scribes and Pharisees?

2. Why do you think some people find Christian faith burdensome?

3. When have you felt that the Christian life is burdensome? What has
   lifted the burden from you?

4. What burdens do we as Christians give to others?

We shouldn't forget that the scribes and Pharisees were not simply
what we would call religious leaders. They were just as much what
we would call social and political leaders or at least the leaders of
popular parties and pressure groups. The problem Jesus identified
is not confined to churches but runs through most modern societies
from top to bottom.

5. In what sense are the scribes and Pharisees "blind" (vv. 16, 19)?

Some have supposed that Jesus, whom we think of as kindly and
loving, could never have denounced anyone, least of all his fellow
Jews, in such sharp tones. It has sometimes been suggested that
these sayings belong to a later age when divisions emerged between
"official" Christianity and Judaism. But that is unnecessary. Jesus

was aware throughout his public career of fierce opposition from parties in Judaism with rival agendas. The present chapter consists of a solemn, almost ritual denunciation of them for their hollow piety and misguided teaching.

6. Jesus accuses the scribes and Pharisees of valuing the gold above the temple and the gift above the altar. They place higher worth on the objects that human beings have brought into God's presence than on God's presence itself. But if the gold and the gifts mean anything, it's because the temple and the altar mean something. And they mean what they mean because of God's promise to be present there.

How could a similar error be made in the church today?

7. *Read Matthew 23:23-39.* How does the external appearance contrast with the inner world of the people Jesus accuses here?

8. Do you find it easier to tend to specific Christian rules or to matters such as justice, mercy and loyalty—and why?

9. Jesus was on his way to draw on to himself all the wickedness of the world, including the wickedness he was denouncing in this chapter and elsewhere, to take their full force on to himself and so to exhaust it. It would be a bad mistake to read a chapter like this as simply a moral denunciation; it would be still worse to read it as a moral denunciation of *somebody else.* That's halfway to committing the very mistake that is being attacked.

Why would authentic prophets of God mentioned in Matthew

23:34-36 be rejected by the people to whom God sends them?

10. What had the Lord longed to do for Israel, and what were the consequences of their refusal?

11. The final sorrowful saying of verses 37-39 makes it clear that the messianic blessings that Jesus longed to bring to Israel can only be received by those who welcome him in faith. "Blessed is the one who comes" is to this day the regular Hebrew way of saying "Welcome" (v. 39). The saying haunts all subsequent telling of Jesus' story. Are we, the readers and hearers, really welcoming the true Jesus, the one who denounces evil and then takes it upon himself in the final great act of love?

What have been some inadequate views of Jesus which you have held, and perhaps still hold?

12. When have you come face to face with the reality of who Jesus is, and how did the encounter(s) affect you?

PRAY

Welcome the Lord into every aspect of your life: family, work, church, community involvements, personal goals, finances, future hopes and fears. Allow him to sort out what is compatible with his will and what is not. Pray that you will never deserve the name *hypocrite* but that your life will be a genuine reflection of the life of Christ.

DANGEROUS TIMES

Matthew 24:1-44

One of the greatest biblical images for God's future is the approaching birth of a baby. The biblical writers draw freely on this well-known experience to speak of the new world that God intends to bring to birth. It's only with images like this that one can speak of God's future. We don't have an exact description of it, and we wouldn't be able to cope with it if we did. What we have are pictures: the birth of a baby, the marriage of a king's son, a tree sprouting new leaves. God's future will be like all these, and (of course) unlike them as well.

OPEN

What is the least expected and most surprising event that has happened to you? Would there have been any way for you to foresee it?

STUDY

1. Much of the Roman Empire was Greek speaking. The Greek word that was used for a state visit by Caesar was *parousia*, an "appearing or presence." It is this word *parousia* which the disciples use when

they ask Jesus about what's going to happen. *Read Matthew 24:1-28.*
What are the chief signs of the Messiah's appearing?

2. What dangers accompany the Messiah's appearing?

3. The disciples wanted to see Jesus ruling as king, with all that that
   would mean, including the temple's destruction and indeed the ush-
   ering in of God's new age. The present age would come to its con-
   vulsive conclusion, and the new age would be born. Well, Jesus says,
   there will indeed be convulsions. But they shouldn't be deceived.
   New would-be Messiahs will appear, but the vindication of Jesus
   himself—his royal *presence* or *appearing* (vv. 3 and 27)—won't be
   that sort of thing. They must hold on, keep their nerve and remain
   faithful. All of this related very specifically to the time between Jesus' public career and the destruction of the temple in A.D. 70.

   Today what are some alarms which tempt Christians to give up and
   be unfaithful to the Lord and each other (v. 10)?

4. How can Christians keep their love from growing cold (v. 12)?

   We too are called to be faithful, to hold on and not be alarmed. We
   too may be called to live through troubled times and to last out to
   the end. We too may see the destruction of cherished and beautiful
   symbols. Our calling then is to hold on to Jesus himself, to continue
   to trust him, to believe that the one who was vindicated by God in

the first century will one day be vindicated before the whole world. We too are called to live with the birth pangs of God's new age and to trust that in his good time the new world will be born.

5. The setting for all this is the sequence of events that will lead to the destruction of Jerusalem described in Matthew 24:15-28. In fact it was forty years before Roman legions surrounded the temple and eventually placed their blasphemous standards there. That was indeed the beginning of the end for Jerusalem, the end of the world order that Jesus and his followers, and their ancestors for many generations, had known.

Jesus describes terrible events to come. What value would there be in his telling his followers these things ahead of time (v. 25)?

6. Consider false messiahs or false prophets you have seen arise in our own time. How do we recognize them as false?

7. Often in the Bible there are passages in which several things have come rushing together as into one short, tight-packed musical sequence. In order to understand them, we have to take them apart and allow them to be heard one after the other. *Read Matthew 24:29-44.* What would be the signs of Jesus' vindication?

8. Jesus said that all these things would happen within a generation (v. 34). That is an extra important reason why everything that has been said in the passage so far must be taken to refer to the destruction of Jerusalem in A.D. 70 and the events that surround it. But I see

no reason why, once we are quite clear about its original meaning, we should not then see the chapter as a pointer to other events, to the time we still await when God will complete what he began in the first century. As we look back to that time, we should also look on to God's still-promised future and thank him that Jesus is already enthroned as Lord of all time and history.

Why would it be difficult to stay alert and ready for the master's appearing (vv. 36-44)?

9. A great many readers have seen in this passage a warning to Christians to be ready for the second coming of Jesus (as promised in Acts 1, for example). Many other readers have seen here a warning to Christians to be ready for their own death. You can read the passage in either of these ways, or both. It is vital, however, to read it as it would have been heard by Matthew's first audience. And there it seems we are back to the great crisis that was going to sweep over Jerusalem and its surrounding countryside at a date that was, to them, in the unknown future, though we now know it happened in A.D. 70 at the climax of the war between Rome and Judea.

What are some typical concerns which distract Christians from awareness of God?

10. What developments in your community have taken your own church by surprise?

11. How can Christians today stay more alert to what God is doing in the world?

PRAY

Pray for discernment among the many appealing but false voices which you hear daily. Pray that you will stay faithful to the Lord no matter what difficulties come. Pray also that you and your fellow Christians will depend on each other and support each other through difficulties.

NOTE ON MATTHEW 24:29-30

For Isaiah (quoted in verse 29 from Isaiah 13:10), and for those who read him in the first century, the one thing this didn't mean was something to do with the actual sun, moon and stars in the sky. This language was well known, a regular code for talking about what we would call huge social and political convulsions. When we say that empires "fall" or that kingdoms "rise," we don't normally envisage any actual downward or upward physical movement. Matthew intends us to understand that the time of the coming of the Son of Man will be a time when the whole world seems to be in turmoil.

What will this coming or appearance of verse 30 actually *be?* Matthew takes us back, in line with so much of Jesus' teaching, to the prophet Daniel again, and this time to the crucial passage in Daniel 7:13. This certainly refers, not to a *downward* movement of this "Son of Man" figure, but to an *upward* movement. The Son of Man "comes" from the point of view of the heavenly world, that is, he comes *from* earth *to* heaven. His "coming" in this sense is not his "return" to earth after a sojourn in heaven. It is his ascension to heaven, his vindication, the thing which demonstrates that his suffering has not been in vain.

22

WISE AND FOOLISH

Matthew 24:45—25:46

Deep within the ancient Jewish tradition we find the book of Proverbs. There, mostly in short sayings but sometimes in more extended pictures, we find in a wealth of detail the contrast between the wise person and the foolish person. Ultimately the wise person is the one who respects and honors God, and the fool is the one who forges him. But their wisdom and folly work themselves out in a thousand different ways in daily life, in business, in the home and village, in making plans for the future, in how they treat other people, in their honesty or dishonesty, in their hard work or laziness, in their ability to recognize and avoid temptations to immorality.

If the living God might knock at the door at any time, wisdom means being ready at any time. Wisdom consists not least in realizing that the world has turned a corner with the coming of Jesus and that we must always be ready to give an account of ourselves.

OPEN

What is the difference between intelligence and wisdom?

STUDY

1. The scene changes once again, as it has done throughout Matthew 24 and will again in Matthew 25; but the underlying drama is the same. *Read Matthew 24:45-51.* What are the expectations of the master?

2. What is the outcome for the faithful slave?

3. Why does the unfaithful slave feel it is safe to misbehave, and how does he get surprised?

The warnings here are held within the larger picture of the gospel, in which Jesus embodies the love of God which goes out freely to all. Of course we shall fail. Of course there will be times when we go to sleep on the job. Part of being a follower of Jesus is not that we always get everything right but that, like Peter among others, we quickly discover where we are going wrong and take steps to put it right. But we can't use God's grace as an excuse for going slack. Even when we don't think we're being watched, we can never forget that much is expected of those to whom much is given.

4. *Read Matthew 25:1-13.* In the Middle East to this day there are some places where the customs at a wedding are quite similar to the ones described here. What makes the difference between the sensible and the silly girls?

5. What are the consequences for both groups?

Even more obviously than the previous parable, this story is rooted in the Jewish tradition of contrasting wisdom and folly—being sensible or silly. Obviously wisdom in this case means being ready with the oil for the lamp, and folly means not thinking about it until it's too late. What matters is being ready, being prepared, being wise, thinking ahead, realizing that a crisis is coming sooner or later and that if you don't make preparations now and keep them in good shape in the meantime, you'll wish you had.

6. What commonly distracts or hinders you from staying ready as a Christian?

7. *Read Matthew 25:14-30.* A *talent* was a unit of money worth roughly what a laborer could earn in fifteen years. Our modern word *talent,* in the sense of the gifts or skills that an individual possesses, is derived from this precisely because of this parable. How does the third servant differ from the first two?

8. A story about a master and slaves, in which the master leaves the slaves with certain tasks to perform and then returns, would certainly be understood in the Judaism of Jesus' day as a story about God and Israel. What gifts had the scribes and Pharisees (and Israel in general) been given?

9. How had they effectively buried them in the ground?

10. Jesus is to be exalted as the ruler of the world, vindicated after his suffering. We are now invited to witness the way in which his just

rule will be exercised. *Read Matthew 25:31-46.* What is the Son of Man's criterion for judgment?

11. The longing for justice, one of the most profound longings of the human race, comes from the Creator God himself. Justice doesn't simply mean punishing wickedness but putting the world right. How will the Son of Man accomplish both halves of justice?

12. Jesus has earlier defined his brothers and sisters as those who do the will of his Father (Matthew 12:50). The likely meaning of this scene is that those who have not followed Jesus the Messiah will be judged in terms of how they have treated the people whom he counts as his family. Instead of the nations being judged on how they had treated Israel, as some Jewish writings envisage, Jesus, consistent with his redefinition of God's people around himself, declares that he will himself judge the world on how it has treated his *renewed* Israel.

How would this passage have been an encouragement to Matthew's first readers?

13. How is this passage an encouragement for you today?

PRAY

Thank God for both his justice and his mercy. Pray about situations in which you need wisdom. Pray also that you will be free from all distractions and petty concerns which keep you from staying prepared for the Lord's coming.

23

The Beginning of the End

Matthew 26:1-56

The death of Jesus of Nazareth is one of the most famous and formative events in human history. It is like a mountainside of sheer rock, compelling and terrifying, which we will attempt to climb. Before you begin to study it line by line, there is a lot to be said for first running your eye right up the wall of rock, for reading the next two chapters of Matthew at a single sitting with the door shut and the telephone turned off. Allow the whole thing to make its proper impact on you.

OPEN

Consider the Gospel accounts of the death of Jesus. What parts of the story have had the most impact on you? What parts do you find most moving? Most shocking? Most mysterious?

STUDY

1. *Read Matthew 26:1-25.* What radical differences do you see between the plotters in the house of Caiaphas and the woman in the house of Simon the leper?

2. Why does Jesus accept the woman's extravagant gift?

3. What is the prevailing mood at this Passover meal as described in Matthew 26:20-25?

4. The figure of Judas is one of the deepest and darkest not only in the Gospels but in all literature. People have written whole books trying to get to the bottom of what he did and why. Why does the betrayal of a friend cut so deeply?

Jesus was going to his death wounded by the wounds common to humanity. Greed, lust, ambition: all kinds of natural drives and desires turned in on themselves rather than doing the outward-looking work the Creator intended them to do.

5. *Read Matthew 26:26-46.* The disciples would have expected Jesus to take the part of the leader at this Passover meal. The first Passover occurred when the angel of the Lord killed the firstborn sons of Egypt but passed over the firstborn of Israel who had sprinkled the blood of a lamb on their doorposts. Pharaoh then chased Moses and the whole nation out of Egypt only to chase after them. Israel escaped through the Red Sea, leaving behind their slavery and going to freedom in their Promised Land. Jesus led the disciples in this annual Passover celebration of God's promised freedom. But in doing so he offered a new direction of thought which, for those who followed him and came to believe in him, took Passover in quite a new direction which has continued to this day.

How does Jesus draw the meaning of the Passover meal onto himself?

6. Imagine that you are there with the disciples in that room. How do you react to Jesus' words in verses 26-29 when he passes round the food and drink?

7. Imagine that you are one of the three disciples there in the garden. When Jesus awakens you those three times, how do you feel? What do you think is going on?

8. Jesus could see, as though it was before his very eyes, the cup (v. 39). This was not the cup of the Last Supper but the cup he had mentioned to James and John (Matthew 20:22-23), the cup the prophets had spoken of, the cup of God's wrath. Here for the second time in the Gospel narrative (the first time being the temptation story in Matthew 4:1-11) we see Jesus fighting in private the spiritual battle he needed to win if he was then to stand in public and speak, and live, and die for God's kingdom.

We have already spoken of the difficulty of fathoming the motives of Judas (vv. 14-16, 21-25). Now we see, with overwhelming pathos, Jesus' last reaction to the traitor as Judas led the arresting party right to the place where he knew they would find him. *Read Matthew 26:47-56.* Even at this moment when Jesus appears helpless, how does he show himself in command of the situation?

9. How does Jesus handle the attempt to defend him (vv. 51-54)?

10. As you have read the account of the betrayal, Last Supper and arrest, what strikes you most about the character of Jesus?

11. Who do you identify with in the story and why?

PRAY

Worship the Lord and thank him for drinking the cup of God's wrath for you. Pray that you will not abandon him when things are tough. Thank him for seeing his mission through to the end.

24

CONDEMNED AND CRUCIFIED

Matthew 26:57—27:44

Have you ever watched two people speaking to each other in different languages, neither understanding the other? Sometimes it's funny,
and effective. Sometimes it's very threatening. I once watched in alarm
as two motorists shouted at each other after a minor traffic accident
which threatened, or so it seemed, to become a major international incident. Both were assuming that the other understood, and were shouting
louder in their own languages (German and Italian, I think) as though
that would get their point across.

As Jesus goes to trial two worldviews came face to face in a dramatic
showdown. These two different ways of seeing and describing the world
gave birth to two different and mutually incomprehensible ways of talking that were bound to meet in head-on collision over the issues of the
temple and messiahship.

OPEN

When have you felt that you were (figuratively) speaking a different
language with someone? What was at the heart of the lack of communication?

STUDY

1. *Read Matthew 26:57-68.* How can you tell that Jesus' conviction was a foregone conclusion?

2. How would you describe Jesus' demeanor before his accusers and the high priest?

Jesus remained silent to the charges until the high priest put him under oath (26:63). Only then does he answer the question of messiahship (26:64) in the same oblique form of *yes* that he gave to Judas (26:25). Perhaps it was a way of avoiding arrogance or apparent selfish pride. But the ringing affirmation which followed made it quite clear that Jesus saw himself and his work in terms of the biblical picture of messiahship.

3. *Read Matthew 26:69—27:10.* Describe Peter in this episode.

4. Denying Jesus is such a sad thing to do. And yet we all do it. Despite the differences of culture and situation, we can see parallels, so close as to be almost amusing, between where Peter was that night and where we may find ourselves.

What sort of questions or challenges from people have led you to keep your association with Jesus inconspicuous?

5. Peter's muddled motives and mixed emotions were no match for the three little questions from a couple of serving girls and a courtier with an ear for a northern accent. They were like small pins stuck into a large balloon, and Peter's world exploded in a roar of oaths and a flood of bitter tears. It speaks volumes both for the accuracy of the Gospels and the humility of the leaders in the early church that Peter's story in all its graphic detail remains there starkly in all four Gospels.

   What similarities and differences do you see between Peter's reaction after denying Jesus (Matthew 26:75) and Judas's reaction when Jesus is condemned?

6. How do the high priests and elders reveal their inner character?

7. The meeting of Jesus and Caiaphas saw a clash of worlds and a failure of communication. The meeting of Jesus and Pilate is the closest the story comes to a showdown between Christ and Caesar, between the King of the Jews and the self-acclaimed Lord of the world. We are invited to watch in awe to see which of the two is vindicated by God. *Read Matthew 27:11-44.* What are the conflicting voices of guilt and innocence in this passage?

8. How is Barabbas a representative of us all?

9. Compare Matthew 27:28-32 and part of the Sermon on the Mount, Matthew 5:39-41. What similarities do you see?

10. It is hard to remember that this is the same Jesus who, days before, was confronting the authorities in the temple, and who, weeks before, was healing people, celebrating with people and teaching them about God's kingdom.

    Imagine that you are a firsthand witness to these events. What goes on in your heart and mind?

11. Never let it be said that the Christian faith is an airy-fairy thing, all about having wonderful inner spiritual experiences and not about the real world. This story takes us to the very heart of what Christianity is all about. Here we meet, close up and raw, the anger and bitterness of the world doing its worst against one who embodies and represents the love of the Creator God.

    As you look at Matthew 27:39-44 where Jesus' public ministry closes, go back and review Jesus' temptations in Matthew 4:1-11 right before his public ministry begins. What similarities do you find between the temptations of Satan and the mockery hurled at Jesus by the onlookers?

12. It is *because* Jesus is God's Son that he must stay on the cross. That is the way the world will be saved. That is how death will be defeated. That is how he will finish the work the Father has given him to do. That is how the Father's delight will be complete.

Jesus leads Israel and all the world through death itself to a new life. He was not simply going to defeat the Romans, or for that matter the chief priests. He was going to defeat death itself. In what ways do we, in Christ, literally and figuratively also pass through death to new life?

PRAY

Pray for a sincere sense of repentance from sin rather than hollow remorse. Offer thanks and praise to Christ for remaining on the cross and completing the work of the Father.

THROUGH DEATH TO VICTORY

Matthew 27:45—28:20

The effect of Jesus' giving of his own life; the example of love, non-retaliation, the kingdom way of confronting evil with goodness; Jesus' taking of the world's hatred and anger onto himself; and beyond all these, the defeat of the powers of evil, the blotting out of the sins of the world, the love of God shining through the dark clouds of wickedness—all of this is now to be seen around the world. It is seen not only in the millions who worship Jesus and thank him for his death, but in the work of healing which flows from it: in reconciliation and hope for communities and for individuals. The world is indeed a different place because of what Jesus did in his death.

OPEN

Recall a moment when you received news that was so good you could hardly believe it. How did you react? What did you do? What did you say? How did the news change your life?

STUDY

1. *Read Matthew 27:45-66*. Consider Jesus' cry of abandonment in verse 46. How are you affected when you read it and hear it in your mind?

2. What are the various—sometimes strange—events which follow Jesus' death in 27:50-54?

3. On the cross the weight of the world's evil really did converge upon Jesus, blotting out the sunlight of God's love as surely as the light of day was blotted out for three hours. Jesus is "giving his life as a ransom for many" (Matthew 20:28). The sin of the "many," which he is bearing, has for the first and only time in his experience caused a cloud to come between him and the Father he loved and obeyed, the one who had been delighted in him.

   How does Matthew rule out in advance the idea that the women would later go to the wrong tomb?

4. How does Matthew rule out the possibility that Jesus' disciples would later steal his body?

5. There was no confusion about the details of Jesus' burial. If you are going to doubt whether Jesus was raised from the dead it must be because you doubt whether the living God could or would do such a thing for Israel's Messiah.

We may imagine that Matthew can hardly wait to take the story into the next chapter where all is revealed. *Read Matthew 28:1-10.* What range of thoughts and emotions do you think go through the women's minds during all these events?

6. "Take away the resurrection of Jesus, and you leave Matthew without a Gospel." How do you respond to that statement?

7. The God who remained silent on Good Friday is having the last word. What God is doing is starting something new. Jesus' resurrection is not about proving some point or offering people a new spiritual experience. It is about God's purpose that must now be fulfilled.

   If the resurrection of Jesus was true, and if people were to start reordering their lives by it, they would be on a collision course with the rest of the world. *Read Matthew 28:11-20.* How do Jesus' enemies fabricate an explanation for what happened?

8. What alternative explanations have you heard for Jesus' resurrection?

9. The ending of Matthew's Gospel in 28:16-20 contains so much that we would do well to slow down in our reading of these final verses and ponder each line, indeed each phrase, to see how they gather up the whole Gospel and pack it tight into the final meeting between Jesus and his followers. What instructions does Jesus give his disciples and therefore us as well?

10. What are the promises which begin and end Jesus' words?

11. Jesus promises "I am with you" every day and to the end. When have you been especially grateful for his presence?

12. Jesus has "all authority" (28:18). It is basic to the most elementary New Testament faith that Jesus is *already* ruling the whole world. What perspective does that give you on the everyday situations you face and on the world as a whole?

PRAY

Consider Jesus' three instructions to make disciples, baptize and teach (28:19-20). Pray about how you and your church can better fulfill that commission. Thank the Lord that he remains with you always and that his authority will have no end.

NOTE ON MATTHEW 27:46

When Jesus cried out, in the opening words of Psalm 22, asking why God had abandoned him, Matthew does not intend us to think, in a comforting sort of way, "Oh, that was all right; you see, it only *felt* like that. Actually, God was carrying him through it all." Part of the whole point of the cross is that there the weight of the world's evil really did center on Jesus, causing something to come between him and the Father. Of course, Psalm 22 goes on to speak of God's vindication of the sufferer and of the establishment of God's kingdom. But that is not Matthew's focus here.

GUIDELINES FOR LEADERS

My grace is sufficient for you.
(2 Corinthians 12:9)

If leading a small group is something new for you, don't worry. These sessions are designed to flow naturally and be led easily. You may even find that the studies seem to lead themselves!

This study guide is flexible. You can use it with a variety of groups— students, professionals, coworkers, friends, neighborhood or church groups. Each study takes forty-five to sixty minutes in a group setting.

You don't need to be an expert on the Bible or a trained teacher to lead a small group. These guides are designed to facilitate a group's discussion, not a leader's presentation. Guiding group members to discover together what the Bible has to say and to listen together for God's guidance will help them remember much more than a lecture would.

There are some important facts to know about group dynamics and encouraging discussion. The suggestions listed below should equip you to effectively and enjoyably fulfill your role as leader.

PREPARING FOR THE STUDY

1. Ask God to help you understand and apply the passage in your own life. Unless this happens, you will not be prepared to lead others. Pray too for the various members of the group. Ask God to open

your hearts to the message of his Word and motivate you to action.

2. Read the introduction to the entire guide to get an overview of the topics that will be explored.

3. As you begin each study, read and reread the assigned Bible passage to familiarize yourself with it. This study guide is based on the For Everyone series on the New Testament (published by SPCK and Westminster John Knox). It will help you and the group if you have on hand a copy of the companion volume from the For Everyone series both for the translation of the passage found there and for further insight into the passage.

4. Carefully work through each question in the study. Spend time in meditation and reflection as you consider how to respond.

5. Write your thoughts and responses in the space provided in the study guide. This will help you to express your understanding of the passage clearly.

6. It may help to have a Bible dictionary handy. Use it to look up any unfamiliar words, names or places. The glossary at the end of each New Testament for Everyone commentary may likewise be helpful for keeping discussion moving.

7. Reflect seriously on how you need to apply the Scripture to your life. Remember that the group members will follow your lead in responding to the studies. They will not go any deeper than you do.

LEADING THE STUDY

1. At the beginning of your first time together, explain that these studies are meant to be discussions, not lectures. Encourage the members of the group to participate. However, do not put pressure on those who may be hesitant to speak—especially during the first few sessions.

2. Be sure that everyone in your group has a study guide. Encourage the group to prepare beforehand for each discussion by reading the introduction to the guide and by working through the questions in each study.

3. Begin each study on time. Open with prayer, asking God to help the group to understand and apply the passage.

4. Have a group member read aloud the introduction at the beginning of the discussion.

5. Discuss the "Open" question before the Bible passage is read. The "Open" question introduces the theme of the study and helps group members to begin to open up, and can reveal where our thoughts and feelings need to be transformed by Scripture. Reading the passage first will tend to color the honest reactions people would otherwise give—because they are, of course, supposed to think the way the Bible does. Encourage as many members as possible to respond to the "Open" question, and be ready to get the discussion going with your own response.

6. Have a group member read aloud the passage to be studied as indicated in the guide.

7. The study questions are designed to be read aloud just as they are written. You may, however, prefer to express them in your own words.

   There may be times when it is appropriate to deviate from the study guide. For example, a question may have already been answered. If so, move on to the next question. Or someone may raise an important question not covered in the guide. Take time to discuss it, but try to keep the group from going off on tangents.

8. Avoid answering your own questions. An eager group quickly becomes passive and silent if members think the leader will do most of the talking. If necessary repeat or rephrase the question until it is clearly understood, or refer to the commentary woven into the guide to clarify the context or meaning.

9. Don't be afraid of silence in response to the discussion questions. People may need time to think about the question before formulating their answers.

10. Don't be content with just one answer. Ask, "What do the rest of you think?" or "Anything else?" until several people have given answers to the question.

11. Try to be affirming whenever possible. Affirm participation. Never reject an answer; if it is clearly off-base, ask, "Which verse led you to that conclusion?" or again, "What do the rest of you think?"

12. Don't expect every answer to be addressed to you, even though this will probably happen at first. As group members become more at ease, they will begin to truly interact with each other. This is one sign of healthy discussion.

13. Don't be afraid of controversy. It can be very stimulating. If you don't resolve an issue completely, don't be frustrated. Explain that the group will move on and God may enlighten all of you in later sessions.

14. Periodically summarize what the group has said about the passage. This helps to draw together the various ideas mentioned and gives continuity to the study. But don't preach.

15. Conclude your time together with the prayer suggestion at the end of the study, adapting it to your group's particular needs as appropriate. Ask for God's help in following through on the applications you've identified.

16. End on time.

Many more suggestions and helps for studying a passage or guiding discussion can be found in *How to Lead a LifeGuide Bible Study* and *The Big Book on Small Groups* (both from InterVarsity Press/USA).